Plague and Pestilence

Plague and Pestilence

A History of Infectious Disease

Linda Jacobs Altman

Enslow Publishers, Inc.

40 Industrial Road	PO Box 38
Box 398	Aldershot
Berkeley Heights, NJ 07922	Hants GU12 6BP
USA	UK

http://www.enslow.com

Library of Congress Cataloging-in-Publication Data

Altman, Linda Jacobs.
    Plague and pestilence : a history of infectious disease / Linda
Jacobs Altman.
        p. cm. — (Issues in focus)
    Includes bibliographical references and index.
    Summary: Traces the battles that societies have waged against
infectious diseases from the Black Death of the fourteenth century
to the Ebola virus of more recent times.
    ISBN 0-89490-957-6
    1. Communicable diseases—Juvenile literature. [1. Communicable
diseases. 2. Diseases.] I. Title. II. Series: Issues in focus
(Springfield, N.J.)
RA643.A48   1998
614.4'9—dc21   98-12677
                                                   CIP
                                                    AC

Printed in the United States of America

10 9 8 7 6 5 4

To Our Readers:
All Internet addresses in this book were active and appropriate when we
went to press. Any comments or suggestions can be sent by e-mail to
Comments@enslow.com or to the address on the back cover.

Illustration Credits: Courtesy of U.S. National Library of
Medicine, pp. 15, 16, 21, 24, 36, 37, 49, 50, 54, 60, 65, 68,
71, 76, 77, 79, 94, 97, 109, 111.

Cover Illustration: Courtesy of U.S. National Library of
Medicine.

Contents

Demons, Miasmas, and Microbes

March 10, 1997, started out as a typical Monday at Del Campo High School near Sacramento, California; busy teachers, crowded hallways, the bray of the morning bell. That afternoon, however, fifteen-year-old Heather Ziese began to feel dizzy and asked permission to go home early. She had a headache and a stiff neck, but no fever. Her family thought she might be coming down with the flu.

Heather went to bed, hoping to go back to school the next morning. During the night, however, her headache and neck pain grew worse, her eyes became sensitive to bright light, and she fell into a restless sleep that bordered on unconsciousness.

At about 3 A.M. Heather's alarmed father bundled her into the car and took her to the hospital. A few hours later, Heather Ziese was dead, the victim of a fast-acting strain of bacterial meningitis.

Meningitis is an inflammation of the membranes that cover the spinal cord. The bacterial meningitis that infected Heather Ziese is swift, virulent (poisonous; very harmful), and contagious. It can be transmitted by direct exposure, such as touching, kissing, or sharing eating utensils. If the infection is diagnosed during the early stages of the disease, it can be cured with antibiotics (a class of drugs that kill bacteria).

Public health authorities went to work to stop the disease from spreading. Anyone who had been in close contact with Heather was treated with antibiotics. The school sent letters to all the students' parents explaining the symptoms of bacterial meningitis and stressing the importance of immediate treatment. Meanwhile, counselors from other schools came to Del Campo to help Heather's friends and classmates deal with their grief.

The story of Heather Ziese's death appeared on the front page of her hometown newspaper, the *Sacramento Bee*. Even people who never knew Heather or her family were stunned by the tragedy. School district representative Christine Olsen summed up community reaction in one single sentence: "Young people aren't expected to die; they're expected to live."[1]

True, young people shouldn't die, but of course, they do. Fast-acting infections can strike even the young and the healthy. In the United States there are one to three cases of bacterial meningitis infection for every one hundred thousand people in the population.[2] According to the National Center for Infectious Diseases (NCID), that translated into 3,243 cases in 1995.[3] Up to 10 percent of the victims die.

Although the United States has been able to prevent large meningitis epidemics (sudden outbreaks that infect many people), other nations have not fared so well. In 1974 a meningitis epidemic in Brazil, which infected more than one hundred fifty thousand people, killed eleven thousand and left another forty-five thousand people with long-term handicaps, such as brain damage, hearing loss, or learning disabilities.[4]

In Africa, epidemics are common in the "meningitis belt." This region stretches across the continent from Senegal to Ethiopia. It includes all or part of fifteen countries and about 300 million people. In 1996 meningitis infected one hundred fifty thousand people, causing sixteen thousand deaths.[5]

Pestilence: The Grim Reality

Meningitis is just one of the many deadly diseases that have plagued humankind. They go by names like Black Death, typhus, cholera, polio, and AIDS.

Germs by the millions, armies of germs, have shaped world history in ways we may hardly realize. They are silent, invisible, and able to reproduce with alarming speed.

In only twenty-four hours one bacterium can multiply into 16,777,220, mutating (changing) as it goes.[6] Over time those changes can make diseases harder to cure and easier to transmit. Germs become resistant to drugs that once killed them, or they develop new modes of transmission. For example, a germ that spreads by direct contact can mutate into an airborne form. Every cough or sneeze from an infected person will then spread germs, infecting more people in a shorter period of time.

In the mid-twentieth century, scientists thought they had conquered contagious diseases. They could prevent many diseases with vaccines and cure many others using antibiotics and other drugs. In addition, water could be purified and objects ranging from kitchen counters to hospital operating rooms could be sterilized (made germ free).

In those optimistic times, every schoolchild knew the story of Alexander Fleming's laboratory accident. In 1928 a small amount of the mold *Penicillium notatum* accidentally fell into a live sample of staphylococci bacteria. To Fleming's surprise, a chemical within the mold killed the staphylococci; he called that unknown substance penicillin.

When penicillin came into general use after World War II, death rates from infectious diseases plunged. Scientists also discovered more antibiotic drugs, which were used to cure a wide range of infections. Between 1945 and 1970, average life expectancy in the United States increased by a full five years. Antibiotics played a major role in this increase.

People and Germs in Prehistory

Two million years ago, give or take a few thousand, prehistoric humans learned to use fire, make simple stone tools, and hunt animals for food. Eating meat introduced more cell-building protein into the human diet. People became bigger, stronger, faster. But the fossil record shows that these advances came at a price. Contact with prey species led to many zoonoses (animal diseases that infect humans). These diseases included encephalitis (a brain disease) and trichinosis (an often deadly intestinal infection).

Other microbes (microorganisms; germs) were unleashed when nomadic (wandering) hunters settled down to become farmers. The Agricultural Revolution, as it came to be called, gave humans better control over their food supply. Instead of foraging for plants, people could grow them in large quantities. Instead of hunting wild game, they could domesticate (tame) food animals such as cattle and sheep.

However, the price for this advance was heavy. Microbes and disease-bearing insects thrived in the standing water of irrigated fields and in the untreated feces used as fertilizer. Runoff from the fields entered the water supply. This brought such diseases as malaria (a mosquito-borne fever) and cholera (a waterborne gastrointestinal infection).

Urban environments became breeding grounds for another class of infections, the zymotics (crowd diseases), which included smallpox, measles, typhus, and scarlet fever. During the Bronze Age, about six thousand years ago, urban populations reached what science historian Arno Karlen calls "a crucial threshold."[7] When large populations live closely together, germs can pass quickly from host to host. Each new victim infects many others.

Demons, Witches, and Deadly Winds

People were terrified by the epidemics because they had no idea of their cause, let alone of a cure. People blamed the outbreaks on everything from demonic possession and miasmas (poisonous emanations from swamps, garbage dumps, or other tainted environments) to witchcraft and the wrath of God.

The ancient Persians, for example, named and described 99,999 disease demons. Some of their writings have survived, like this description of "Al," the demon of scarlet fever:

> Would you know Al? She seems a blushing maid,
> With locks of flame and cheeks all rosy red.[8]

Demons were evil, supernatural beings. Reasoning with them was useless, and punishing them was impossible. Would-be healers could only hope to drive the demons away by begging, bribing, and threatening them.

Witches, on the other hand, were human. During

the medieval era (roughly A.D. 1300–1600), elderly women who dabbled in folk medicine were often charged with witchery. In times of epidemic, they were often blamed and killed by the terrified and superstitious populace.

Yet in good times, people asked these so-called witches for everything from love charms to herbal ointments and healing teas. Some of the remedies actually worked to relieve symptoms if not to cure diseases: mint tea could soothe a "sour stomach," for example. Other treatments were useless, though, such as wearing a leather shoestring around the neck to cure a cough, or this remedy for a fever: running "thrice round a willow-tree at sunrise, crying, 'The fever shall shake thee, and the sun shall warm me.'"[9]

Cultures that blamed demons or witches for their ills rarely thought victims deserved what happened to them. Cultures that worshiped a righteous god, on the other hand, believed that diseases were sent to punish sinners.

This practice of blaming the victim has never quite disappeared from Western culture. When the venereal (sexually transmitted) disease syphilis was recognized in the fifteenth century, many people thought it was God's punishment for sexual sin. The same would be said of AIDS in the twentieth century.

Naturalistic Explanations

The Greek physician Hippocrates (c.460–377 B.C.) laid the foundation for medical ethics with the

Hippocratic oath—a vow still taken by doctors in the United States and many other parts of the world. He also laid the foundation for medical science by attempting to explain disease in natural terms.

Hippocrates believed that diseases were caused by environmental conditions, not gods or demons. Marshy waters and summer heat brought fevers and intestinal disorders; cold winters ushered in respiratory ailments; and hot winds brought everything from asthma to epilepsy.

Though his conclusions were wrong, his methods of study were not. Hippocrates taught the importance of observation and investigation—two cornerstones of the scientific method. In his book *On Airs, Waters, and Places*, Hippocrates wrote:

> Whoever wishes to investigate medicine properly, should proceed thus: in the first place to consider the seasons of the year. . . . Then the winds, the hot and the cold. . . . We must also consider the qualities of the waters, for as they differ from one another in taste and weight, so also do they differ much in their qualities. . . . From these things [the physician] must proceed to investigate everything else.[10]

Six hundred years after Hippocrates, the Roman physician Galen (A.D. 129–199) studied the structure and functions of the human body. Galen wanted to dissect (cut apart for examination) human bodies to see how the organs worked, but the Roman religion forbade it. Instead, he had to make do by studying the bodies of animals. Galen's research laid the groundwork for the sciences of anatomy (the

The Greek physician Hippocrates (c. 460–377 B.C.), author of the Hippocratic oath, believed that diseases were caused by environmental conditions, not gods or demons.

Galen became Imperial Physician of Rome in A.D. *168. His studies of human anatomy established a scientific foundation for medicine.*

study of physical structure) and physiology (the study of bodily functions). His hands-on experimentation would later become instrumental in the development of the scientific method.

It would be several hundred years before the scientific method would produce answers about infectious disease. Scientists did not discover that germs cause diseases until the late nineteenth century. It took longer still to understand how those germs spread through whole populations and to develop drugs that could kill invading microbes. Gradually, painfully, humankind sorted fact from fiction and transformed medicine from an uncertain art into a more precise science.

2

The Black Death

Modern etiology (the science that deals with the causes of diseases) recognizes four major types of disease transmission: airborne, waterborne, by direct contact, and through vectors (insects or other creatures that carry germs from one species to another). Each type has caused its share of epidemics, none more famous than the flea-borne bubonic plague of the fourteenth century.

Later generations would call it the Black Death. People who lived through those terrible times knew it as the Great Dying or the Pestilence. By any name, the

18

plague that swept through Europe, North Africa, and parts of Asia in the fourteenth century was the most devastating epidemic in history.

It struck Europe in October 1347, brought into the port of Messina, Sicily, by a fleet of Genoese trading ships. The fleet had come from Kaffa, a seaport on the Crimean peninsula in modern-day Ukraine. The traders were fleeing an army of Tatar warriors who had laid siege to the city. (The Tatars were an ethnic group that spoke Turkish and followed the Muslim religion.)

In the midst of the siege, a terrible sickness had struck the Tatar soldiers. So many of them had died that the survivors had no time to bury them. The bodies were stacked like cords of firewood against the city walls. When the traders slipped out of Kaffa during a lull in the fighting, they must have shivered at the grisly sight.

Unfortunately, the fleeing traders probably had no way of knowing that the common black rat was the host animal for the plague-bearing fleas. Infected rats must have left Kaffa on the Genoese ships. By the time the fleet reached Messina, all the crew were dead or dying; and the rats slipped unnoticed to the shore.

The Great Dying

The Black Death involved the three forms of plague: bubonic, referring to painful lymph node swellings called buboes; pneumonic, an airborne form that first attacks the lungs; and septicemic, which is called "blood poisoning."

The classic sign of bubonic plague is the appearance of buboes in the groin and armpits, which ooze pus and blood. Victims bleed under the skin until they are covered with dark blotches. They have soaring fevers. In the fourteenth century, plague was considered a death sentence. More than half the victims died, usually within four to seven days and always in agony.

In the case of the pneumonic form of plague, every cough or sneeze from an infected person expels germs into the air for others to inhale. This form attacks the lungs, causing "an overwhelming pneumonia" with "high fever, cough, bloody sputum, [and] chills."[1] It kills swiftly, often in less than two days.

Septicemic plague is "a direct invasion of the blood stream without lymph node involvement."[2] When plague attacks the blood stream, germs flow through the entire body, multiplying as they move. The germs reproduce so rapidly that the victim's own blood becomes toxic (poisonous). People have been known to die within hours after displaying the first symptoms of septicemic plague. Even today, the fatality (death) rate for this form is high. In the fourteenth century, it was virtually 100 percent.

When plague reached Europe, it first struck port cities and then followed the trade routes both by sea and land. It raged through Italy into France and the British Isles. It was also carried over the Alps to

Not everyone abandoned plague victims to their fate. Here, a group of people take care of stricken comrades.

Switzerland and eastward into Hungary and Russia. Everywhere it went, hundreds of thousands fell sick and died. In Tournai, Belgium, the death toll was so high that authorities outlawed funeral processions and the ringing of death bells. They even forbade the wearing of mourning dress, except for widows. Without such rules, life would have become an endless procession of black-garbed mourners, marching to the tolling of the bells.

A resident of Siena, Italy, described how mass death blunted normal grief: "And no bells tolled, and nobody wept no matter what his loss because almost everyone expected death. . . . And people said and believed, 'This is the end of the world.'"[3]

Even last confessions had to be set aside; there weren't enough priests to hear them. Many a plague victim died in fear of hell because no priest was present to perform last rites. Pope Clement VI resolved the problem by granting absolution (forgiveness of sin) to all who died of plague.

Seeking Answers, Placing Blame

People of the fourteenth century could not imagine that an invisible thing called a germ could cause the miseries of plague. Some thought the Black Death was the wrath of God, poured out upon a sinful world. Some blamed the stars and looked to astrology for answers. Others blamed an earthquake that hit Italy in January 1348, just as plague was making its way from Messina (on the island of Sicily) to the European mainland.

Only a few thought of quarantines (separation of infected people from the general population) or public sanitation measures, but even they did not suspect contagion. They blamed miasmas or believed that plague victims were dangerous in some mysterious way. For example, Guy de Chauliac, physician to the royal court of France, thought a person could become infected just by looking at someone with plague.

When plague first appeared in Venice, Italy, authorities there put together a plan to stop it from spreading. They made strict rules about handling corpses, placed controls on immigration, and ordered a forty-day quarantine on arriving ships. The quarantine kept sailors aboard their ships, but it did not prevent black rats from coming ashore.

The Italian city of Pistoia regulated the public marketplace, set standards for burial of plague victims, and outlawed travel to plague-stricken areas.

The longer plague continued to spread, the more people were willing to believe that this terrible pestilence was God's punishment to a sinful world. This being the case, the Tournai town council set itself the task of raising the morals of the community. To gain favor with an angry God, citizens gave up gambling, drinking, gluttony, greed, and working on Sunday. There was no drop in the death rate, and the reforms did not last for long.

Desperate people needed something—or someone—to blame for their hardships. So they did what people have always done in such situations: They looked for the stranger whose ways seemed different and dangerous. They found lepers, who were victims of an "evil" illness; and Muslims, whose religion and culture were alien to Christian Europe. Most of all, though, they found Jews, who stubbornly kept to themselves and rejected the teachings of Christianity.

In southern France, rumor spread that Jews had poisoned the wells to kill Christians and destroy their religion. Pope Clement VI issued an order forbidding attacks upon Jews. He pointed out that

Many priests tending plague victims died along with their patients. This engraving was part of a tribute to these men who put compassion for others before their own survival.

plague killed Jews as readily as Christians; blaming them for the horror made no sense.

The terrified population was not listening. The hatred had gone too far for that, the fear too deep. In the German city of Mainz, Christians rounded up twelve thousand Jews and burned them alive. The people of Basle (now Basel), Switzerland, built a house on an island in the Rhine, forced the whole Jewish community into it, and then burned them alive. There were other massacres in other places, but still the plague continued to rage.

A Company of Sinners

Plague entered Germany in the autumn of 1348. It was there that a cult named the Brotherhood of the Cross, commonly known as the Flagellants, began its grim pilgrimages. Flagellants punished themselves for the sins of humankind, hoping to convince God to stay his hand.

The Flagellants moved silently through the countryside of central and southern Germany, a snaking procession of some two hundred to one thousand cowled figures. Their robes were marked with red crosses, front and back. Upon coming into a town, they would gather in the marketplace where everyone could see them. Their dark robes came off, leaving only a linen skirt for modesty's sake. Then out came the scourges, which one witness described as "a kind of stick from which three tails with large knots hung down. Through the knots were thrust iron spikes as sharp as needles which projected about the length of a grain of wheat or sometimes a little more."[4] The Flagellants would move in a circle, whipping themselves, sobbing, chanting, and bemoaning their sins.

As the Flagellant cult grew, it spread to Hungary, Poland, and the Low Countries (present-day Belgium, the Netherlands, and Luxembourg). Groups of Flagellants made their way to France and even to England. As the sect grew, its members became more militant. The Brotherhood mocked the Catholic Church and defiled (ruined) altars. Anyone who opposed them was evil, they said; only they could save the world from the Great Dying.

The Flagellants finally went too far in their defiance of the Church. Pope Clement VI outlawed the Brotherhood in October 1349. With the awesome authority of the pope against them, the Flagellants lost their influence. Towns that had once welcomed them began to bar the gates. By the end of 1350 the Flagellant processions had stopped.

Later Outbreaks

The plague receded for a time after wiping out at least a third of Europe's population. But every ten to twenty years, plague struck again. There were half a dozen more outbreaks before the end of the fourteenth century. These later epidemics were not as widespread, but wherever they hit they were deadly.

The result was social upheaval. People became obsessed with death. Poets wrote eulogies (statements of high praise) for the dead. Musicians composed dirges (funeral hymns). Artists painted endless versions of the *danse macabre* (the "dance of death," in which a black-robed skeleton leads victims in a grim procession toward the grave).

Plague left people doubting the teachings of the Church, the goodness of God, and the authority of kings. The turmoil was painful and confusing. No one could say where it would lead, but one thing was certain: European civilization would never be the same.

3

Predators at Large

The European Renaissance, or "rebirth," of the fifteenth and sixteenth centuries is remembered as a time of cultural and scientific growth. As the scientific method of direct experimentation gained acceptance, biology and medicine made important strides.

Belgian physician Andreas Vesalius (1514–1564) did what Galen had been forbidden to do: He dissected human bodies to learn about their structure. Vesalius's dissections of human cadavers modernized the science of anatomy.

Physiology got a similar boost from

the work of British physician William Harvey (1578–1657). His studies of physical processes showed that blood circulates through the body rather than moving one way, as Galen had supposed.

The microscope was invented around the end of the sixteenth century, probably by Dutch lensmakers Hans and Zacharias Janssen. Pioneer biologist Antoni van Leeuwenhoek (1632–1723) used the new instrument to discover blood cells and bacteria.

In the midst of these scientific advances, though, epidemics continued to kill. Diseases such as typhus, syphilis, and measles laid waste to whole populations. England's last great outbreak of bubonic plague devastated London in 1665.

Cycles of Infection

The science of epidemiology (the study of epidemics) began with Thomas Sydenham in seventeenth-century England. Through detailed observation, Sydenham identified and described diseases such as scarlet fever, malaria, and smallpox. His descriptions became a tool for diagnosis (determining which disease is present in a given case). He then went on to investigate epidemics by the same careful process.

Sydenham's methods set the tone for the study of epidemics. Modern epidemiologists still rely upon observation and description to do their work. When investigating an outbreak, they identify the disease, isolate the germ that caused it, and trace the outbreak back to its source. For example, an outbreak of food poisoning might be traced back to contaminated (tainted, poisoned) meat at a single restaurant. The next steps are to stop the disease from spreading and to provide treatment for people who are already sick.

Scientists have learned that infectious diseases follow a pattern of emergence, infection, adaptation, and retreat. The microbes that cause a disease can remain dormant (inactive) for hundreds of years. They might survive in an animal or insect reservoir (a species that carries a harmful organism). Their exact origin, however, is often unknown.

Newly emergent diseases strike hard. They rip through virgin populations (those never exposed to a particular disease) with overwhelming speed and ferocity, causing the death rate to soar. Those who survive develop antibodies (disease-fighting agents produced by the immune system) that make them more resistant to that particular infection.

But while humans are adapting to the unfamiliar germ, the germ is also adapting to them. Like all forms of life, microbes must reproduce in order to survive as a species. Killing the host too quickly actually works against that process. Science historian Arno Karlen compares it to the relationship between predators (animals that kill for food) and the animals they hunt: "If predators gobble up all available prey, they will eventually starve and disappear."[1] If infected people die too quickly, the microbes have less time to reproduce and spread through the population. Less time, therefore, means fewer victims. Each generation of germs becomes smaller than the one before it, and the epidemic drops below a sustainable threshold. When the microbes can no longer propagate (reproduce and transmit) themselves, they retreat to their reservoir and become dormant until the population grows large enough to sustain a new outbreak.

From Epidemic to Endemic Disease

Over time, this cycle of infection and retreat changes an epidemic disease into an endemic one, meaning it is present in a community at all times. Each time a population is exposed to the disease, more people develop antibodies. The result is fewer and milder infections. Through this process, many dreaded killers become routine childhood diseases.

Measles is the classic example of this process. Measles is caused by an airborne virus (a class of pathogen or bacteria so small it cannot be seen with an ordinary microscope). It probably originated three or four thousand years ago when people began crowding into cities.

Ancient sources did not distinguish measles from other rash-producing infections, such as smallpox, chicken pox, and scarlet fever. However, sixteenth-century records, compiled by historian Karlen, show what measles could do to virgin populations:

> Measles followed smallpox to the new world. In 1529, a measles epidemic in Cuba killed two-thirds of the natives who had survived smallpox. Two years later it had killed half the people of Honduras, ravaged Mexico, spread through Central America, and attacked the Incas.

The death toll was appalling, Karlen writes. "Whole cities and tribes [were] wiped out, cultures and languages lost. Corpses lay scattered in fields and heaped in silent villages."[2]

Pestilence and War

Epidemic diseases have affected the outcomes of many wars. During a war between the Greek city-states of Athens and Sparta (begun in 431 B.C.), an epidemic killed one third of Athens' population. The Greek historian Thucydides (c.460–c.400 B.C.) lived through these events. From his description in The History of the Peloponnesian War, the disease was smallpox or a similar rash-producing infection.

Thucydides described fever and vomiting followed by "reddish . . . pustules [blisterlike skin eruptions]."[3] Victims could not stand the touch of clothing or bed linen. In delirium (extreme mental confusion) they wandered naked through the streets until they fell over dead: "The bodies of dying men lay one upon another, and half-dead creatures reeled about the streets and gathered round all the fountains in their longing for water," according to Thucydides.[4]

Although some people did survive the illness, many of them went blind or lost fingers and toes to gangrene, an infection that kills living tissue. Others lost their memory.

Athens' social structure became unhinged in the wake of the plague. Honest folks turned to thievery in order to survive, the good-natured became hostile, the brave became fearful. Most everyone became obsessed (preoccupied; overly concerned) with death. Weakened from within and attacked from without, Athens fell to Spartan troops in 404 B.C.

In the fifteenth century, typhus and syphilis burst upon the scene. Both were well suited to battlefield conditions. Typhus is carried by lice, which thrive in crowded, filthy quarters, such as military barracks. Soldiers, weakened by poor nutrition and forced to disregard personal hygiene, are especially vulnerable to lice-borne disease. Syphilis is transmitted by sexual contact. When it first appeared, prostitutes were a normal part of military life on the battlefield. Hundreds of prostitutes would follow an army, camping where they could be available to the troops.

The first recorded outbreak of typhus occurred in 1489, when the Spanish Army besieged the Moorish city of Granada. The epidemic began with the arrival of hired troops from the Balkans. These soldiers must have carried infected lice. Within days of their arrival, a vicious infection raged through the Spanish camp. Headaches and swiftly rising fevers were its first symptoms, followed by gastrointestinal upset and foul-smelling skin ulcers that could develop into gangrenous (rotting) sores.

Victims became delirious and then sank into a stupor from which most of them would never awake. It was this stupor that gave the disease its name, from the Greek *typhos*, meaning "haze" or "smoke." While only three thousand Spanish troops died in battle during the siege, seventeen thousand succumbed to typhus. This hidden death toll was typical of warfare throughout human history; armies of unseen microbes decided the outcome of many a battle.

The Secret Sin

Like typhus, syphilis appeared as a terrifying and, usually, lethal new infection. Its victims died in agony, with symptoms that made other people turn away in disgust: open sores, rotting body parts, and mindless delirium. "In contrast to the disease's slow and well-mannered progress today," writes Canadian science writer Andrew Nikiforunk, "fifteenth-century syphilis turned a healthy person into a leprous-looking mess in a couple of weeks and buried him or her within a year."[5]

The true origins of syphilis are shrouded in mystery. Some historians argue that it descended from a twenty-thousand-year-old African zoonosis. Others place its beginnings in the New World. They argue that the crews of Columbus's ships brought the spirochete (bacteria with corkscrewlike form) back to Europe after one of the voyages to the New World.

The first recorded outbreak of syphilis occurred in 1495, after King Charles VIII of France besieged the city of Naples, Italy. The soldiers in the king's army were mercenaries (foreign soldiers who serve for pay rather than patriotism). These men, and the prostitutes who followed their camps, came from all over Europe. When they went home, the disease went with them.

It did not take long to figure out the connection between syphilis and sexual activity. People quickly jumped to what they thought was the obvious conclusion: Syphilis was God's punishment for sexual misbehavior. Medical efforts to cure or prevent the disease were, therefore, sinful: Only chastity (refraining from all immoral sexual activity) would do. Five hundred years later, a new generation of moralizers would say much the same thing about AIDS.

The Great Plague of London

England's last great battle with bubonic plague, in 1665, is one of the best-documented epidemics in history. This is largely due to a book by English author Daniel Defoe (1660–1731). Defoe is best remembered for the classic *Robinson Crusoe*, but he also wrote *A Journal of the Plague Year*.

The journal was written in 1722, more than fifty years after the plague it describes. It is therefore not a firsthand account, nor is it a scholarly history. It is what we call today a docudrama. The experiences of individuals are fictionalized, but facts and figures are generally accurate.

Defoe gave a naturalistic explanation of the epidemic at a time when most people believed it was God's punishment for sin. However, he did this in a way that religious people could accept; the plague was "no less a judgment [from God] for its being

The plague that devastated London in 1665 brought back horrifying images of the Black Death. Stricken people died

View of the manner of burying the dead at Berlin at Holy well mount during the dreadful PLAGUE *in 1665*

in the streets while death wagons dumped victims into mass graves.

under the conduct of [earthly] causes and effects," he wrote.[6] In other words, God only had to let nature take its course. The plague itself was "more than sufficient to execute the fierceness of Divine vengeance."[7]

The concept of contagion was still unknown in 1665. Even people who believed that disease was a natural process were likely to blame miasmas. According to Defoe, however, a few learned men believed that the breath of infected people could transmit plague. Some of them even held that something *in* the breath might be the true culprit.

Defoe offered a colorful description of this idea. Plague "might be distinguished by the [victim's] breathing upon a piece of glass, where . . . living creatures [might] be seen by a microscope, of strange, monstrous, and frightful shapes, such as dragons, snakes, serpents, and devils, horrible to behold."[8]

Even without knowing about germs, people showed an intuitive awareness of contagion. When plague struck, those who could afford to leave London fled for their lives. Those who could not leave avoided contact with infected people.

Some plague victims showed their awareness of contagion in a particularly gruesome way, deliberately exposing others to their disease. Diarist Samuel Pepys described infected people leaning out their windows to breathe into the faces of passersby, "to carry contagion to them."[9] In Portsmouth, England, which was also ravaged by plague, Commander

Thomas Middleton of the Royal Navy told of plague victims throwing their contaminated bandages through the windows of healthy people.

The Great Plague of London took a stunning toll; 68,596 deaths were officially attributed to plague. The actual total may have been nearer to 110,000, however, since unreported deaths were common in seventeenth-century London.[10] Thousands of poor slum dwellers died unnoticed, as did Quakers, Jews, and others who did not make a practice of reporting deaths to the parish church.

A Grim Picture

Death surrounded everyone and everything in London. There was hardly enough time to bury the victims, let alone keep accurate records. Defoe speaks of death carts rumbling through the midnight streets, and the "horrible cries and noise the poor people would make at their bringing the dead bodies of their children and friends out [to] the cart, and by the number one would have thought there had been none left behind."[11]

British historian Walter Bell, working from manuscripts in the archives of St. Margaret's church in London, provides an equally grim picture:

> When darkness fell over London and on till past midnight at the height of the visitation, often the streets resounded with the cry, that hushed all who heard it, "Bring out your dead!" From some of the dark houses marked with the Plague cross came no response. The bearers, leaving the dead cart in the street, entered, and searched about

with lighted candles. In the ghastly rooms they learnt why there had been no answer to their cry. It was not unusual to find that the whole household had perished.[12]

Such horrifying scenes were common in times of pestilence. The cycle of epidemic repeated itself with measles, smallpox, typhus, and many other diseases. In time, when these diseases became endemic in Europe, people tended to forget how deadly they had once been. The exploration of the New World would provide a frightening reminder.

4

Brave New Worlds

European explorers and settlers brought more than a new way of life to the Americas; they also brought a host of new microbes. Diseases that had become endemic in Europe turned deadly among people who had never been exposed. Smallpox, measles, mumps, typhoid, and other Old World diseases decimated whole tribes with frightening efficiency.

The Legacy of the Explorers

After Columbus landed on the island of Hispaniola during his second voyage in 1493, local people started to die of a

41

virulent infection. Some historians say it was smallpox; others believe it was a kind of swine influenza that jumped species. Whatever the nature of the microbe, the results are undisputed: Before the epidemic, more than one million people lived on the island; afterward, only ten thousand survived.

When Hernán Cortés attacked the Aztec capital of Tenochtitlán (present-day Mexico City), he had a force of three hundred men against a population of three hundred thousand. In spite of such overwhelming odds, Cortés conquered the city within three months.

Neither skill nor weaponry accounted for the improbable victory—it was smallpox. One member of the Spanish force had a mild case when he landed in Mexico. The Spaniards, with their generations of exposure, were immune to the worst ravages of the disease. The Aztecs were not.

By the time the conquistadores marched into the vanquished city, half its population was dead and the survivors were too sick and frightened to resist. Friar Toribio Motolinia recorded the devastation in his journal. The Aztecs, he said, died "in heaps, like bedbugs. . . . In many places it happened that everyone in a house died, and, as it was impossible to bury the great number of dead, they pulled down the houses over them in order to check the stench that rose from the dead bodies, so that their homes became their tombs."[1]

From Mexico, epidemics spread south to the Mayan empire of Central America and north all the way to the Great Lakes. By the time Hernando de Soto arrived in the Mississippi Valley in 1539, there was nothing left of the legendary mound builders who had once lived there. The explorer found nothing but a grim wasteland of deserted towns with houses stacked full of corpses.

Smallpox reached Massachusetts in 1617, well ahead of the Pilgrims, who landed there in 1620. It came with earlier explorers, probably by way of Nova Scotia, Canada. More epidemics followed in 1630 and again in 1634, killing thousands of American Indians. The minister Cotton Mather claimed that God had sent these epidemics to rid the land "of those pernicious creatures to make room for better growth."[2] By way of "proof," he pointed out that the disease killed American Indians by the thousands but did not even make the Europeans sick.

In the end, European germs were responsible for more destruction of the native peoples than European gunpowder. Over a period of four centuries, epidemic diseases wiped out as much as 90 percent of the American Indian population.[3]

Death by Inches

Both leprosy (now called Hansen's disease) and tuberculosis are "wasting" diseases that slowly destroy the tissues they infect. Both caused epidemics in the ancient world; a description of tuberculosis appears in the work of Hippocrates, and the Bible discusses leprosy.

Aside from their long histories, the two diseases appear to have little in common. Tuberculosis is transmitted in the minute droplets of moisture expelled during coughing, while leprosy, which is less contagious, requires close physical contact with an infected person. The symptoms of the two diseases are entirely different.

In actuality, though, the two microbes are connected in unexpected ways. Microbiologists (scientists who study the life processes of microorganisms) have discovered that *Mycobacterium leprae*, the bacterium that causes leprosy, and *Mycobacterium tuberculosis* are so similar to each other that they cross-immunize: Each disease gives sufferers resistance to the other. According to Arno Karlen, this cross-immunity "is not automatic and absolute, but the presence of either disease does greatly lower the odds of catching the other."[4]

Tuberculosis primarily infects the lungs, but it can also attack other parts of the body. For example, scientists have found tubercular decay in the spinal columns of Egyptian mummies dating from 2400 B.C.

In 400 B.C., Hippocrates noted that it was the most widespread disease of the age. He called it *phthisis*, from the Greek word *phote*, meaning a body shriveling in intense heat. Later generations called it consumption, from the Latin *comsumere*, meaning "wasting away." The term *tuberculosis* ("full of tubercles"—the bacilli that cause the disease) and the shortened *TB* did not become common until the twentieth century.

By any name, tuberculosis has been one of history's worst killers. Unlike other diseases, it did not rage through an area leaving piles of corpses behind; instead, it killed more slowly, over months and even years. The tuberculosis germ can enter a person's body and lie dormant for years. Once the disease becomes active, symptoms include extreme tiredness, loss of weight, and fever. There is a deep, hacking cough that expels contagious droplets into the air. Victims waste away until their lungs collapse and they can no longer breathe.

Although some people did survive tuberculosis, a diagnosis of the dreaded white plague, as it was sometimes called, was widely regarded as a death sentence. Even today, treatment is a lengthy and expensive process. Effective drugs became available in the 1950s, but many people did not have access to them. This continues to be a problem, especially in developing countries where large numbers of people live in grinding poverty. In the late 1990s, there were 8 million new cases of tuberculosis and 3 million deaths from the disease every year.[5]

"Leper" Means Outcast

Leprosy probably originated in India or East Africa more than four thousand years ago. It infects and slowly destroys skin and nerves. The skin becomes thickened and folded, especially on the face. This gives victim an odd, lionlike appearance that many people find frightening. Nerve damage can cause loss of feeling, especially in hands and feet. It may also affect motor functions, causing an awkward, stumbling gait.

Throughout human history victims of this disfiguring illness have been regarded with particular horror. The leper, with his shambling walk and twisted appearance, seemed like something out of a monster legend. People considered lepers frightening and dangerous; they believed that lepers were cursed by God.

Long before anyone understood the nature of contagion, lepers were singled out for strict quarantine. They had to wrap themselves in bandages and heavy cloaks, with hoods drawn over their faces. They carried a bell, which they rang whenever they approached other people.

A religious order known as the Knights of St. Lazarus (Lazarus was the patron saint of lepers) established a network of lazar houses or leprosariums. Lepers could live in these sanctuaries, away from the society that hated and feared them. By the end of the thirteenth century, there were nineteen thousand lazar houses in Europe alone.

Leprosy had all but disappeared from Europe by the end of the fourteenth century, though. The reason for its disappearance has long puzzled scientists and historians. Some think that the Black Death wiped out Europe's lepers. People who were already weakened by leprosy would be vulnerable to the plague. If a large number of lepers died from plague, there would not be enough of them left to continue spreading leprosy.

Another idea goes back to the connection between leprosy and tuberculosis. Epidemics of these two diseases never seem to occur at the same time; as one begins to rise, the other declines. Why does this happen? How is it connected to the cross-immunity between *Mycobacterium tuberculosis* and *Mycobacterium leprae*? Answers to these questions could lead to new methods for prevention and cure of both diseases.

The African Connection

Anthropologists (scientists who study human origins and evolution) have proved that humankind originated in tropical Africa. So did many of the most dangerous microbes known to medical science. These African diseases came to the New World with the first slave ships, which began their grisly trade in the early seventeenth century.

Europeans paid a high price for enslaving Africans. The captives carried diseases like yellow fever and an especially severe form of malaria. This African malaria was far deadlier than the strain that was already established in the New World. Both strains are carried by mosquitoes, and both produce symptoms that include high fever, chills, and sweating. The difference occurs within the blood stream. In the African strain, infected red blood cells clump together. This disrupts blood flow throughout the body. Lack of blood flow in turn damages organs and nerves.

In the New World, African malaria first appeared in Central and South America. The moist, tropical climate provided ideal breeding conditions for the mosquitoes that carried the disease. Every puddle of stagnant water became a breeding ground.

The yellow-fever mosquito is highly adaptable to its environment. It can breed in freshwater containers such as barrels and casks, and it can also survive in cooler temperatures. This means that yellow fever can spread into temperate zones during the summer, causing short-lived but deadly epidemics.

Yellow fever takes its name from the jaundiced pallor of the victim's skin, which is a symptom of liver malfunction. Yellow fever strikes with headache and fever, followed by chills, muscle pains, and vomiting. There is often bleeding in the stomach and intestines. Since this blood has not been oxygenated (combined with oxygen) by the lungs, it is dark in color. The result is "black vomit."

Those who die from yellow fever usually do so within six to nine days of the first symptoms. Those who survive may require weeks to regain their strength, but they acquire lifelong immunity to the disease.

One of the worst epidemics in American history hit Philadelphia late in August 1793. At the time, Philadelphia was the capital of the United States and home to government officials and other distinguished citizens. Many of them fled to the

Y YELLOW FEVER

A medical alphabet published in 1837 used this startling portrayal of yellow fever to illustrate the letter Y.

While others fled Philadelphia during the yellow fever epidemic of 1793, Dr. Benjamin Rush stayed to treat the victims. He noticed an unusual number of mosquitoes that summer but did not connect them with the epidemic.

countryside when the epidemic began. President George Washington, his family, and his staff packed up and went to the Washington home in Mount Vernon. Even respected physicians left town, aware that they could neither cure the victims nor stop the spread of infection. Within a month the epidemic of 1793 had killed 15 percent of Philadelphia's population.[6]

In the ongoing search for the cause of disease, the Philadelphia epidemic became a platform for the miasmatic view. Dr. Benjamin Rush traced the outbreak to a cargo of spoiled coffee that had been left to rot on the docks: "The first cases of the yellow fever have been clearly traced to the sailors of the vessel who were first exposed to the effluvia [offensive fumes] of the coffee," he wrote, and added that "their sickness commenced with the day on which the coffee began to emit its putrid [rotten] smell."[7]

Dr. Rush also noticed an unusual number of mosquitoes that summer, but he never connected them with the epidemic. He thought that mosquitoes and yellow fever just happened to thrive in similar conditions. It therefore seemed natural that cleaning up decaying matter and standing water would help to control both the insects and the disease.

The theory of miasmas is an excellent example of how wrong answers can sometimes lead to right actions. Cleaning up miasmatic environments actually did reduce the spread of disease. This success would trigger new ideas and new approaches to the problem of epidemic disease.

5

Turning Points

After the yellow fever epidemics of the late eighteenth century, the war against contagious disease began to pick up momentum. By the mid-1850s there had been a few minor triumphs and at least one major disaster: Asiatic cholera, a new crowd disease, came out of India to kill millions around the world. On the positive side, the first vaccine was discovered, a major epidemic was traced to its source, and new ideas about sanitation began to prevent diseases years before Louis Pasteur's germ theory finally helped explain their causes.

Edward Jenner and the Milkmaids of Gloucestershire

Edward Jenner (1749–1823) was a country doctor with an interest in scientific research and a practiced eye for seemingly insignificant details. Had he spent his life in London or any other large city, he might never have noticed a peculiar fact: Milkmaids did not contract smallpox. No matter how bad the epidemic, they did not get sick. Neither did anyone else who had contracted cowpox, a mild infection that was endemic in cattle. Sooner or later, most everyone who worked around dairy herds would catch cowpox. They would break out with pimplelike sores, feel sick for a few days, then recover completely. Thereafter, they were immune to both diseases.

Why not infect people with cowpox to confer immunity to the more dangerous disease, Jenner thought. He took pus from the arm of a milkmaid who was sick with cowpox and rubbed it into a small cut on the arm of a healthy eight-year-old boy. The boy soon came down with cowpox, just as Jenner had expected. After the young patient recovered, Jenner took another, far riskier step: He deliberately infected the boy with smallpox.

No modern researcher would take such a risk until making innumerable trials in cultures (tissue cells cultivated in artificial environments) and in animal subjects. In Jenner's time there were no protocols for medical research. The procedure seemed sensible, so Jenner carried out the

Edward Jenner created the first vaccine in history after noticing that milkmaids who contracted cowpox during their work were immune to smallpox.

experiment. Fortunately, it worked; the boy did not contract smallpox. Considering the magnitude of this finding, one would expect other physicians to have begun inoculating their patients immediately. Instead, they reacted with skepticism, disinterest, or sometimes outright hostility.

These physicians had no framework for understanding the process of conferring immunity; the germ theory of disease was still decades away. Neither Jenner nor anyone else could say *why* inoculation worked, only that it did. When the chief surgeon of prestigious St. Thomas's Hospital in London began using Jenner's technique, it gained a measure of credibility. Within a few years, acceptance widened as more people realized that Edward Jenner had found the means to conquer one of the deadliest maladies known to humankind.

Cholera and the Great Sanitary Awakening

The origin of Asiatic cholera is uncertain. Some historians believe it first appeared twenty-five hundred years ago in the Ganges Delta of India. Others claim a more recent beginning. They link the disease to an 1817 epidemic that began in Calcutta and quickly became a full-fledged pandemic. Merchant ships carried the disease to China, Japan, and Southeast Asia. Slave traders transmitted it to East Africa and the Arabian Peninsula.

Cholera is a fast-spreading, deadly disease that is caused by a waterborne bacillus (a rod-shaped bacterium). Once swallowed, the cholera bacillus breeds within the intestines. It releases a toxin (poison) that causes diarrhea and vomiting. Victims lose so much body fluid that they become dehydrated, suffering a severe loss of water from all organs and tissues. Their muscles cramp, the soft tissues of their faces wither and shrink from lack of water, and their lips turn sickly blue. Cholera kills 20 to 50 percent of the people it infects, some within a matter of hours, others within a few days.

After a second pandemic struck Europe in the early 1830s, English social reformer Edwin Chadwick decided to study sanitary conditions in London. Chadwick was convinced that filth created the miasmas that caused cholera and other diseases. In crowded London, he found ample support for this belief. He examined the water supply, sewage treatment, and garbage disposal systems, as well as household filth. The relationship between dirt and disease was exactly as he had expected: the dirtier the environment, the higher the number of victims.

Fellow sanitationist William Farr, a physician with a flare for statistics, analyzed the data. It seemed to prove Chadwick's theory that filth formed lethal miasmas. In 1842, Chadwick released his monograph *Sanitary Condition of the Labouring Population of Great Britain*.

In 1848, Chadwick became commissioner of Great Britain's first board of health. By cleaning up the garbage, purifying the water, and providing proper sewage facilities, his public sanitation program reduced the spread of infection. For Edwin Chadwick, that was enough.

"Blessed was the rugged common sense of the nineteenth century!" exclaims historian Charles Winslow. He writes:

> The theory [of miasmas] was indeed incomplete. "Filth," as has been said, "is not the mother but the nurse of disease." Yet the theory . . . had enough truth in it to work. When the sanitary reformers cleaned up the masses of putrefying filth through which our great-grandfathers moved, the epidemics of typhoid and cholera and typhus and dysentery actually ceased. The miasmatic theory was the first generalization of [disease causation] to be actually—and on a world-wide scale—justified by its fruits.[1]

Cholera and the American Frontier

Cholera reached the United States at a time when the young nation faced wholesale changes and runaway growth. Immigration, industrialization, and westward expansion shaped American society in beneficial ways. But these developments also made America an incredibly rich environment for microbes of every description. Tuberculosis and a dozen other diseases raced through the cities, especially the poverty-stricken tenement neighborhoods where immigrants struggled to get a foothold in the New World. Cholera dogged the westbound wagon trains, leaving a trail of shallow graves from the embarkation points along the Missouri River to the shores of the Pacific Ocean.

In the spring of 1849, when thousands of eager adventurers set out for the goldfields of California, cholera spread upriver from New Orleans to the outfitting towns where wagon companies took on supplies and prepared for the prairie crossing.

Journalist Bayard Taylor, whose chronicles provide a unique view of life and death in those wide, wild days, recorded the grim truth about the epidemic's toll on the pioneers:

> The cholera, ascending the Mississippi from New Orleans, reached St. Louis about the time of their departure from Independence, and overtook them before they were fairly embarked on the wilderness. The frequent rains of the early spring, added to the hardship and exposure of their travel, prepared the way for its ravages, and the first three or four hundred miles of the trail were marked by graves. It is estimated that about four thousand persons perished from this cause. Men were seized without warning with the most violent symptoms, and instances occurred in which the sufferer was left to die alone by the roadside, while his panic-stricken companions pushed forward, vainly thrusting to get beyond the influence of the epidemic. Rough boards were planted at the graves of those who were buried near the trail, but there are hundreds of others lying unmarked by any memorial, on the bleak surface of the open plain and among the barren depths of the mountains.[2]

Taylor's comment about panicked attempts to "get beyond" the epidemic hint at some underlying idea of contagion. The journal of Sarah Royce, another gold rush pioneer, goes into some detail about efforts to disinfect her family's wagon after a cholera death: "The fact was at once recognized that close contact with the disease for several hours, had exposed us to contagion, and had also made necessary the disinfecting of our wagon and all its contents."[3]

This disinfection process shows a growing acceptance of sanitation as a means of controlling disease. Unfortunately, no one suspected that something living in "clear" water could be the agent of such destruction. Without that information, the pioneers could neither prevent nor cure cholera; they could only hope for the best and try to outrun or outlast the killer disease.

John Snow and the Broad Street Pump

When a cholera outbreak hit the Soho section of London in 1854, a young doctor named John Snow began to suspect its causes, and he started an investigation that was remarkable for its time. Instead of theorizing about the problem, Snow went into the field to study it. The results of that study would make history.

Snow carefully mapped the location of every case of cholera, noting where the victim fell sick. A pattern soon emerged, revealing an unmistakable cluster of fatalities in the area around the Broad Street pump. The conclusion was obvious to Snow: Somehow, the water from that pump was infecting people with cholera.

Rather than waste time trying to prove his case

London physician John Snow made medical history when he tracked a cholera outbreak to its source: contaminated water from the famous Broad Street pump.

to a skeptical public, Snow convinced local authorities to remove the handle from the pump. The epidemic ceased soon afterward. In later research, the doctor tracked more outbreaks, methodically connecting each to its source.

"Snow is renowned among epidemiologists because of his pioneering thinking in doing research," writes Robert Ginsberg in *Nation's Health*. "The story is also retold because of the public health principles it illustrates. . . . Snow cut off the problem at its source and did not simply minister to individual victims. And he took the initiative to address the problem before all the details of causation could be shown."[4]

Even without a theoretical foundation, Snow's results not only provided a new weapon against cholera but also furthered the cause of the hygiene movement. Governments throughout Europe and North America patterned their own health departments after the British model. New York City created a municipal health board in 1866; the United States government soon followed with a national agency.

Snow's methodology was as important to the advancement of medical science as his results. His detailed observations and standardized methods for recording and analyzing raw data transformed epidemiology from an eccentric activity into a respected science. Every microbe hunter who tracks the source of a new epidemic begins with methods similar to those John Snow established in 1854.

The story of the doctor and the Broad Street pump has passed into scientific folklore. In 1992 the Westminster City Council honored the innovative doctor with a monument on Broad Street—a replica of the original pump, with a plaque explaining its significance.

6

Stalking
the Enemy

"Seeing is believing" goes the old saying. For most of human history, people have accepted that as true. They might make exceptions for demons and other supernatural beings, but not for invisible "germs" that could kill millions. Such an idea was beyond all common sense. Perhaps that's why germ theory was such a long time coming.

Microbiologist Hans Zisser ranks "seeing is believing" as one of the most dangerous of the "adages and proverbs which tend to become the philosophy of the thoughtless. . . . For thousands of years,

63

wise men believed that the earth was flat and that the sun moved around the earth—because they could see with their own eyes that these things were so."[1]

But medicine made great strides in the etiology and diagnosis of disease between 1860 and 1880. The work of people like Edwin Chadwick and John Snow led to the public health movement. That work also posed new questions about contagion; questions the miasmatic theory could not answer.

Scientists such as Louis Pasteur, Joseph Lister, and Robert Koch set out to find those answers. They looked beyond what "everybody knew." They tested their theories and replaced misinformation with facts that could be proved in laboratory experiments.

Louis Pasteur and Germ Theory

Louis Pasteur (1822–1895) was the son of a tannery operator in Dole, France. In 1847 he received his doctorate from the École Normale in Paris. Two years later he was appointed professor of chemistry at Strasbourg.

The work that would lead him to the germ theory of disease began with a paper on the fermentation of wine. Through a series of laboratory experiments, Pasteur proved that the yeast that converted sugar into alcohol was a living microorganism—a "germ" he called it. Different germs had different effects on sugar. For example, one germ turned sugar into lactic acid, the bitter acid present in sour milk; another turned it into alcohol. The meaning of these findings was obvious to Pasteur: If invisible organisms caused

Louis Pasteur (1822–1895), whose pioneering work produced the germ theory of disease, a vaccination for the cattle disease anthrax, and the heat-treating sterilization process that bears his name, pasteurization.

one biological process, then they could cause others—including infectious diseases.

Between 1860 and 1861, Pasteur showed that harmful organisms in food and beverages could be destroyed with heat. Pasteur discovered that wine could be sterilized by heating it to 57.2 degrees Celsius (135 degrees Fahrenheit).

Milk can be sterilized at 71.7 degrees Celsius (161 degrees Fahrenheit). After heating, it is quickly cooled to prevent new contamination. This procedure, called pasteurization, has saved millions of people from serious infections.

Louis Pasteur continued his research on germs. On May 29, 1878, he stunned the French Academy of Sciences with a paper titled "Germ Theory and its Applications to Medicine and Surgery."

Pasteur understood the impact of his work. Coming to terms with germ theory was not easy for many people. Scientists who had accepted the miasmatic theory saw their lifeworks disproved. Ordinary people struggled to understand how organisms too small to be seen could kill whole populations. "If it is a terrifying thought that life is at the mercy of . . . these minute bodies," Pasteur wrote, "it is a . . . hope that Science will not always remain powerless before such enemies."[2]

Pasteur believed what he said. Building on the foundation of germ theory, he went on to develop vaccines against anthrax (a deadly cattle disease) and rabies ("mad dog" disease), both of which are a threat to humans. Pasteur's work set the standard for future progress in medical research.

Joseph Lister and Sterile Surgery

In 1857, the same year that Pasteur wrote his paper on fermentation, English surgeon Joseph Lister (1827–1912) presented his own study, titled "An Essay on the Early Stages of Inflammation."

Lister was the fourth of seven children in a well-to-do Quaker family. He received his medical degree in 1852, then became an assistant to Professor James Syme at the University of Edinburgh.

In this job, Lister saw the terrible conditions existing in British hospitals of the day. Nearly 50 percent of the surgical patients and those who had open wounds died of infection. Most people believed that these infections were caused by miasmas that naturally developed in and around hospitals. Lister suspected it was something in the wound.

In 1865, he read about Pasteur's heat-treating process for killing germs, and his suspicion turned to certainty. He began experimenting with different chemicals to discover their antiseptic (germ-killing) properties. The most efficient antiseptic he found was carbolic acid, a by-product of coal tar. Lister used the acid to wash wounds and surgical incisions, disinfect bandages, and clean operating rooms. The results were impressive. Lister's methods cut the death rate from hospital infections by more than half.

In spite of this success, Lister's 1867 paper on

Joseph Lister's principles of antisepsis not only made surgery safer but also led to better hygiene in food preparation, laundry, and personal care.

antiseptic surgery was largely ignored by other doctors. They simply were not interested in a procedure based on the new and controversial germ theory. However, the success of Lister's methods eventually forced them to change their minds. The impact of those methods was not limited to operating rooms. The idea of preventing infection by controlling germs also revolutionized the treatment of infectious disease.

Robert Koch, the Microbe Finder

German physician Robert Koch (1843–1910) also built upon germ theory. His work isolated and identified the specific germs that caused various diseases.

Koch was a country doctor in Wollstein, Germany. Working with nothing but a microscope and his own determination, Koch isolated the anthrax germ and studied its life cycle. As the final proof of his work, he used the newly identified bacterium to produce the disease in laboratory mice.

Koch's achievement threw the scientific world into an uproar. For the first time, someone had linked a specific microbe to a specific disease. When Koch presented his work at the University of Breslau in 1876, the distinguished professor Julius Cohnheim called it "the greatest discovery ever made in bacteriology."[3]

From this early discovery, Koch developed the research procedures that later became known as Koch's postulates. These postulates outlined the scientific method for identifying a germ and connecting it to a particular disease. Koch's procedure held that

(1) the germ responsible for causing a disease must be present in every case of the disease;

(2) it must then be grown in controlled laboratory conditions;

(3) the laboratory-grown organism must produce the disease in otherwise healthy susceptible animals;

(4) the germ must then be found in the newly infected animal.

Koch went on to make other great scientific discoveries. He isolated the staphylococcus bacterium, a principal cause of surgical infections, and developed a better way to grow bacteria for laboratory experiment. He improved the microscope lens and light source and took the first microphotographs of a germ. And in 1882 he discovered the tuberculosis bacillus.

Koch later discovered tuberculin, a substance produced by the tuberculosis bacillus. Tuberculin was not a cure for tuberculosis—as Koch had hoped it would be—but it was an excellent diagnostic test. When injected under the skin, tuberculin will cause redness to appear if the person has tuberculosis or has had it in the past. The tuberculin test is still in use today with only minor changes.

A short time after discovering the tuberculosis germ, Koch found the bacillus that causes cholera and proved that it is transmitted in contaminated

Mass inoculations for smallpox began as early as 1850 and were commonplace by the end of the century. Lining up for "shots" was a new and bewildering experience for many.

water. He went on to develop a vaccine against the cattle disease rinderpest. He also studied bubonic plague in India, and he discovered that the tsetse fly transmitted the germ of African sleeping sickness.

The Practicalities of Survival

In the 1840s, botanist (a scientist who studies plant life) Hermann Brehmer found out that he had tuberculosis. Rather than sit back and wait to die, Brehmer went to Tibet, hoping that the dry mountain air would slow the progress of his disease.

It did better than that; it cured the disease. When Brehmer returned home, his doctor examined him and found no trace of the disease. This experience prompted Brehmer to leave botany and study medicine. When he had completed his studies, he concentrated on the care—and possible cure—of tuberculosis patients. He built a sanatorium in the Swiss Alps, where fresh air, good nutrition, and minimal exertion would give patients a chance to heal.

This sanatorium treatment could not help everyone, though. Fresh air, good food, and bed rest had little effect on patients with advanced cases of tuberculosis. But people in the beginning stages of the disease had a much better chance, and many were cured just as Brehmer himself had been.

The first sanatorium in the United States was at Saranac Lake in upstate New York. It was founded by physician Edward L. Trudeau, who himself was infected with tuberculosis. Other sanatoriums followed. The Montefiore Home for Chronic Invalids in Westchester County, New York, began as a tuberculosis sanatorium. It later expanded to accept patients with cancer, syphilis, kidney disease, and other diseases that were considered incurable.

Thousands of consumptives bypassed the sanatoriums of the East and headed to the wide open spaces of the West. Some went to Colorado for the fresh mountain air; others settled in southern California for the year-round sunshine. "Southern California . . . was nothing but a giant sanatorium," writes Ronald Reese in *History Today* magazine.

> Invalid villages made up of long rows of tents and makeshift shacks grew . . . around many Western and Southwestern towns and cities. The shacks were little more than screened porches just large enough for a bed, a washstand, and the few belongings of its resident "lunger," "cougher," or "hacker." Frontier language was uncompromising.[4]

By 1880, consumptives made up one third of the population of Colorado, with thirty thousand in Denver alone.

By the end of the nineteenth century, medical science had begun to change society's attitude toward epidemic disease. Instead of accepting epidemics as unavoidable, people were looking for methods of prevention. No longer were they resigned to being helpless victims of unknown and uncontrollable forces. They expected answers, and they expected cures. New generations of researchers built upon the work of scientists like Pasteur, Lister, and Koch to find those answers.

7

Adventures in Medical Detection: 1900–1950

During the first half of the twentieth century, public health agencies and medical researchers continued to fight disease on all fronts. Massive mosquito abatement projects all but eliminated yellow fever and malaria in Cuba and Panama. New vaccines provided immunity to diseases that once ravaged whole populations. In America, education and public sanitation projects began to cut the death rate. Even with improvements in hygiene and health care, though, epidemics were more likely

74

to begin in overcrowded immigrant slums than in prosperous middle-class neighborhoods.

America's Immigrant Menace

This fact wasn't lost on many Americans. In the long tradition of blaming the stranger for everything from epidemic disease to moral decay, some native-born citizens looked askance at the immigrants who poured into the country around the turn of the twentieth century. Between 1880 and 1924, over 23 million people left their homelands to seek a new life in America.[1] They came mostly from southern and central Europe. Settling in American cities, they crowded into dirty, disease-ridden tenements as they struggled to get a foothold in a land that considered them alien and quite possibly dangerous.

Whenever an epidemic broke out in an immigrant neighborhood, prejudice and bigotry followed in its wake. Some people were always ready to blame the victims rather than the disease. Immigrants were inferior, these people said; immigrants were more susceptible to disease because they had lower standards of cleanliness. In the mood of the times, even respectable scholars expressed opinions that today would be considered bigoted. A Columbia University professor had this to say about Italian immigrants: "Huddled together in miserable apartments in filth and rags, without the slightest regard to decency or health, they present a picture of squalid existence degrading to any civilization and a menace to the health of the whole community."[2]

Visiting nurses, ready to make their rounds in poor immigrant neighborhoods.

Navy physician Manly H. Simons declared that poor Jewish neighborhoods produced "the greatest proportion of the distorted forms and minds, the beggars, tramps, burglars and other perverts who make life burdensome and fill our prisons with criminals, our asylums with insane."[3]

Neither of these authors furnished any evidence to substantiate their claims. These were flat-out false assertions, designed to arouse fear and hatred toward strangers. Equally inflammatory statements were made about Poles, Greeks, Portuguese, and any others whose appearances or customs seemed odd to established Americans.

From this prejudiced stance, it was only a small step to blaming one immigrant group or another for specific outbreaks of disease. Jews were branded as carriers of tuberculosis because the stereotypical Jewish immigrant looked consumptive—thin and somewhat pale. Italians were blamed for one of the earliest polio outbreaks simply because the first case occurred in a heavily Italian neighborhood.

Fortunately, there were those in the field of public health who took a more enlightened view of immigrants and their health problems. In New York and other cities, visiting nurses went from tenement

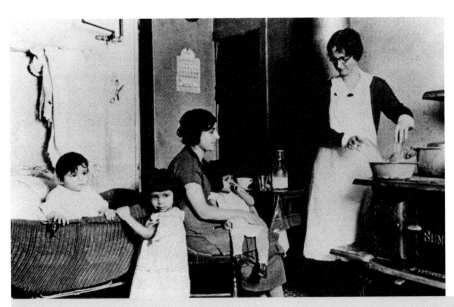

A visiting nurse shows a mother how to sterilize baby bottles at home.

to tenement caring for the sick, educating new mothers about hygienic child care, and making sure that people of all ages were properly immunized against a host of once-deadly diseases.

Public health physicians and research scientists worked together to make advances in diagnosis and treatment. In 1898 a team of dedicated experts began one of the most ambitious projects in medical history, the conquest of yellow fever.

Targeting a Killer

When United States troops occupied Cuba in 1898 during the Spanish-American War, they ran up against yellow fever, which routinely killed seven hundred fifty people a year in the city of Havana alone.

Unlike during the Philadelphia epidemic of 1793, this time scientists had the tools to isolate the cause of the infection and to devise a method for combating it. In 1900 a special commission headed by Army doctor Walter Reed went to Cuba to conduct an investigation.

Nearly two decades earlier, Dr. Carlos J. Finlay of Havana had theorized that a particular species of mosquito carried the disease. No one had listened to him at the time, but the Reed Commission took a new look at Finlay's ideas. To test the theory, they enlisted volunteers who allowed themselves to be bitten by infected mosquitoes. On August 24, 1900, commission member Dr. James Carroll became the first to be infected. He fell sick four days later, and

Walter Reed, the young Army doctor whose daring research in Cuba proved that mosquitoes transmit the yellow fever virus to humans.

for three days after that he hung between life and death. Carroll recovered, but others were not so lucky.

Dr. Jesse Lazear of the commission was infected intentionally, according to some sources—accidentally, according to others. He died on September 25, 1900. Several months later, nurse Clara Maass allowed herself to be infected. Despite all efforts to save her, she died on August 14, 1901.

Through the self-sacrifice of these people, Walter Reed's group not only proved that mosquitoes transmit the infection but also identified the type of pathogen (disease producing agent) that causes the disease: It was a mysterious organism called a filterable virus.

Russian scientist Dmitri Ivanovski had discovered the first filterable virus in 1882 while studying a disease of tobacco plants. The cause of the tobacco disease was a pathogen so small that it could pass through bacteria-trapping filters and still infect healthy plants. Five years later, German scientist Friedrich Löffler found that another filter-passing germ caused foot-and-mouth disease in cattle.

Walter Reed and his team were the first to identify a filterable virus as the cause of a human disease. In the laboratory, that was an exciting discovery. In the field, however, it did not count for much: Recognizing the pathogen was a far cry from curing the disease.

Like John Snow taking the handle off the Broad Street pump, the commission devised a practical solution to the problem: mosquito control. Under the direction of future Army surgeon general William Gorgas, teams of workers killed mosquitoes and cleaned out their breeding areas. As the mosquitoes disappeared, so did the yellow fever. The Cuban epidemic was over in a matter of months.

The Strange Saga of Typhoid Mary

Another dramatic case of medical detection began in the summer of 1906 at a rented vacation cottage on Long Island, New York. An unexplained outbreak of typhoid fever struck six people in the household of eleven. The owners of the property hired George Soper, a sanitary engineer known for his epidemiological studies of typhoid fever.

In checking possible sources of contamination, Soper learned that the family had hired a new cook, who had arrived just before the outbreak and had left three weeks after it. The idea that an apparently healthy person could carry disease was not yet well understood, but Soper had a hunch.

The cook, thirty-eight-year-old Mary Mallon, had worked for eight different families since 1897; seven of them had experienced unexplained outbreaks of typhoid fever. Soper found Mallon working for a family on Park Avenue. Try as he might, he could not convince her to give samples of feces, blood, and urine for testing. Lacking the authority to force compliance, Soper turned over his data to the New York City Health Department.

Health inspector Dr. S. Josephine Baker had no

better luck in persuading Mallon to cooperate. The only alternative was to take her into custody—and that proved to be a decidedly hazardous undertaking. On orders from the head of her department, Dr. Baker went to Mallon's house with an ambulance and three policemen. "We were to . . . get the blood and urine specimens and, if Mary resisted, we were to take her to the Willard Parker Hospital, by force if necessary," Dr. Baker recalled in her autobiography, *Fighting for Life*.

> Leaving the ambulance at the corner, I placed one policeman around the corner, another in front of the house and with the remaining one I went to the basement door. Mary was on the lookout and peered out, a long kitchen fork in her hand like a rapier. As she lunged at me with the fork, I stepped back . . . and so confused matters that, by the time we got through the door, Mary had disappeared.[4]

After a lengthy search, Dr. Baker found the infuriated cook hiding in a closet under the stairwell.

> Once the door was opened [Mary] wasted no time. She came out fighting and swearing, both of which she could do with appalling efficiency and vigor. I made another effort to talk to her sensibly . . . but it was of no use. . . . There was nothing I could do but take her with us. The policemen lifted her into the ambulance and I literally sat on her all the way to the hospital; it was like being in a cage with an angry lion.[5]

Against her will, Mallon was tested for the typhoid bacillus. The results confirmed George

Soper's instincts: Mallon's bowel movements were "a living culture of typhoid bacilli."[6] She passed the organisms to others through her cooking.

Mallon refused to believe that something called a germ could make her dangerous to anyone who ate her food. As she pointed out many times, she never had typhoid fever.

Quarantine

Dr. Baker and many others tried to explain about healthy carriers, but the idea was new and confusing even to them. To Mary Mallon it was downright foolish. Because she would not agree to quit working as a cook, Mallon was sent to the city's quarantine facility on North Brother Island. There she remained until February 19, 1910, when she signed an agreement promising "that she would never again take any position that involved handling food."[7]

In March 1915, Dr. Baker investigated an outbreak of typhoid fever at the Sloane Maternity Hospital: "I went up there one day and walked into the kitchen. Sure enough, there was Mary earning her living in the hospital kitchen and spreading typhoid germs among mothers and babies and doctors and nurses like a destroying angel."[8]

Mallon was sent back to North Brother Island, this time for good. She lived in a private cottage and worked in the laboratory at the island's Riverside Hospital. She died at that hospital on November 11, 1938, after twenty-six years of forced quarantine.

The story of Typhoid Mary raises serious

questions about individual liberty and public health. Placing her in permanent quarantine was not an ideal solution, but health authorities of the day regarded it as necessary to protect the public.

In the age of AIDS and HIV, the problem of the apparently healthy carrier takes on fresh urgency. Nobody seems to know exactly how to handle it. In 1996 historian Judith Walzer Leavitt examined the Mallon case in detail. She concluded that

> Mary Mallon's captivity and the stories of other individual sufferers and carriers demonstrate the need for policies that . . . put the least restriction on individual lives [while still] protecting the public's health. . . . The conflict between . . . civil liberties and public health will not disappear, but we can work toward developing public health guidelines that recognize and respect the situation . . . of individual sufferers.[9]

The Summertime Scourge

Although some authorities believe that polio dates back to ancient times, most consider it a "distinctly twentieth-century disease."[10] The first outbreak in the United States struck Rutland County, Vermont, in 1894. But it was not until 1916 that polio became a widespread epidemic. That year saw twenty-seven thousand cases in twenty-six states, with more than six thousand deaths. New York City alone had 8,927 cases.

Polio is caused by a virus that flourishes in warm weather, spreads through direct contact, and attacks nerve cells in the spinal cord. It is sometimes called infantile paralysis because it primarily strikes children and young people. "Among neurological [nervous system] diseases . . . polio is unique in its ability to cause rapid and often permanent paralysis," writes Yale professor of surgery Sherwin B. Nuland. It was not unusual "to see a child admitted in the morning with mild weakness of one leg who then went on to total neck-down paralysis by sundown."[11]

Polio could kill by paralyzing vital body systems, such as the muscles needed for breathing. Respiratory failure meant almost instant death until Professor Philip Drinker of Harvard University invented the iron lung in 1927.

This bulky machine looked like something out of Dr. Frankenstein's laboratory. Along with leg braces and the wheelchair, it became a grim symbol of the disease during the polio scares of the 1930s, 1940s, and early 1950s.

American research scientist Jonas Salk (1914–1995) developed an injectable, killed-virus vaccine (viruses grown in a culture medium then killed with a special chemical). In 1955 the U.S. Public Health Service approved the Salk vaccine for use in the United States. Five years later, an oral vaccine developed by virologist Albert Sabin (1906–1993) received approval.

There is still no cure for polio once it strikes, nor is there a foolproof treatment to restore damaged nerve tissue. In the United States and other developed nations, mass immunization has almost eliminated polio. This is not the case for the rest of the world, however, where every year brings another one hundred thousand cases of this preventable disease.[12]

The Pandemic Nobody Remembered

They called it "Spanish influenza" because it was said to have come from Spain. In 1918, it stormed through a defenseless world. In just nine months it killed between 20 and 40 million people, mostly young adults in the primes of their lives.[13] This was an epidemiologist's nightmare: a fast, deadly, and incurable airborne disease that defeated every effort to contain it.

In spite of its ferocity, the pandemic was quickly forgotten once it passed. World War I, not Spanish influenza, defined those years. Even medical histories tend to pass over the subject. Books tend to focus on medieval death carts heaped with corpses, on smallpox and leprosy, and on tragic invalids wasting away with tuberculosis. Somehow the flu doesn't seem very dramatic.

Even doctors of the time discounted the flu's seriousness. In the early stage of the outbreak, misdiagnosis was common. Doctors simply could not believe that a minor disease like influenza could cause such terrible symptoms. American Studies professor Alfred W. Crosby explains:

> The abruptness of the onset of the disease and the degree to which it overwhelmed the patient . . .

seemed far too extreme to be [caused by] influenza of any kind. After all, influenza, flu, gripe, grip—whatever you called it or however you spelled it—was a homey, familiar kind of illness: two or three days in bed feeling downright miserable, a week or so feeling shaky, then back to normal.[14]

At Camp Devens, an Army base near Boston, the first influenza victim showed up at the base hospital on September 7, 1918. He had a high fever and a headache, and he could barely sit up. His symptoms were so severe that doctors believed he had meningitis. But his other symptoms were more flulike: cough, dripping nose, and sore throat. The next day a dozen men showed up with the same symptoms.

By September 12, the hard-pressed medical staff had made a diagnosis. They were facing a new form of influenza, one that struck hardest at healthy young adults and tended to settle in the lungs, causing deadly pneumonia.

What organism caused this monstrosity of a disease? In 1918, scientists could go no further than to say that it was a virus. Years later, after virology (the study of viruses) had advanced far enough, researchers studied frozen tissue samples from the 1918 outbreak. The killer virus, however, had not survived the freezing process. It was never identified, nor has it reemerged.

Alan Hampson of the World Health Organization believes that Spanish influenza was probably a combination of two strains that joined to create a new, more deadly pathogen. When this killer flu struck, entire towns took sick and whole families died.

Doctors, nurses, and grave diggers worked round the clock and still could not keep up with the epidemic. No one really knows how many people were stricken, but more than 21 million victims died.

Those who recovered were not disfigured or disabled by their bout with the disease. The pandemic passed, the dead were buried, and life went back to normal. People were soon behaving as if nothing so terrible would ever happen again. They were wrong.

8

The Age of AIDS

They called him Patient Zero—the first known case of a new disease. His name was Gaetan Dugas, and the disease that would not only claim his life but ultimately define it was Acquired Immune Deficiency Syndrome (AIDS). Nobody had heard of AIDS before the early 1980s. This new infectious disease crept up on a thoroughly unprepared world. AIDS was so deadly, it looked to be the real-life equivalent of the fictional Andromeda Strain: a doomsday organism that could wipe out humankind as surely as nuclear holocaust.

89

"Something's Going Around . . ."

In the summer of 1980, Gaetan Dugas had surgery to remove a strange purplish spot from underneath his ear. It was cancer, the doctor said, but it was more puzzling than dangerous.

The young flight attendant had somehow contracted Kaposi's sarcoma (KS). It was a rare form of skin cancer that usually occurred only in elderly Jewish and Italian men. Victims lived with the cancer for years, decades even, until they finally died of something else. Dugas ignored the swelling in his lymph nodes and the bone-weary exhaustion that overcame him every now and then. None of it would slow him down; he had too much living to do.

In San Francisco, Los Angeles, and New York—cities with large homosexual communities—Kaposi's sarcoma and a host of other strange diseases began showing up with disturbing frequency. Doctors saw increases in the numbers of cases of FUO (Fever of Unknown Origin), swollen lymph nodes, rampant fungal infections, and a rare and deadly strain of pneumonia known as Pneumocystis carinii.

In November 1980, Los Angeles immunologist Michael Gottlieb examined a young man who was stricken with candidiasis (a thick, frothy yeast infection commonly called thrush) of the throat and Pneumocystis carinii pneumonia. Since both diseases were linked to immune system malfunctions, Gottlieb arranged to have a T cell count taken of the patient's blood.

T cells had only recently been discovered; they

are a special kind of white blood cell that plays a key role in immune responses. Helper T cells turn the immune system on to destroy invading pathogens, while suppressor T cells turn the system off when the threat has passed.

Gottlieb's patient did not have any helper T cells in his blood. This was more than strange, this was deadly. Without the immune system, the human body has no defense against disease organisms. The result would be multiple infections, with one piling on top of another until the body itself just shut down.

If the immune disorder itself was contagious, the world could be facing a new horror that would make all the epidemics of history pale in comparison.

By the end of 1980, fifty-five Americans had been diagnosed with infections related to immune system breakdown, and four had died. A year later the death toll was up to seventy-four, and it was clear that this new syndrome (group of symptoms occurring together) had come to stay. By January 1982, it even had a name: Gay Related Immune Deficiency (GRID).

Morals and Public Health

The name made the disease somehow more real, but it also triggered a backlash against the victims. By its very definition, GRID was a disease of homosexuals, a group that was hated and feared by many people. Some ultraconservative religious groups said that

GRID was the vengeance of God, sent to punish perverts and sinners.

It had all been said before. "The searing droplets of this cruel sickness fall on those who are hot with love and dirtied with lust; it is a punishment for their misdeeds and their shameful desires," wrote French poet Jean-Baptiste Lalli about a syphilis epidemic in 1629.[1]

Syphilis was almost as much a death sentence in the seventeenth century as AIDS became in the twentieth. In 1910, German chemist Paul Ehrlich (1854–1915) announced a "magic bullet"—a drug he called Salvarsan (from the word salvation). It was the first chemical agent developed to kill one specific microbe, the spirochete that caused syphilis. Some people argued against making the drug available, saying that human beings had no right to interfere with the God's judgment.

In the 1980s, AIDS activists encountered similar attitudes when they publicized safe-sex guidelines and established programs to distribute condoms to anyone who wanted them. Later, when they learned that shared hypodermic needles could transmit the AIDS virus and they offered clean needles to drug addicts, they met even greater resistance. Many moralists said, Tell homosexuals to stop all sexual activity; tell addicts to quit taking drugs. Anything more would amount to an endorsement of immoral behavior.

Within the homosexual community itself, many people could not come to terms with the reality of

AIDS. They were not eager to take preventive measures, such as using condoms. Moralizing from outside the gay community and resistance from within delayed public health measures that might have slowed the progress of the AIDS epidemic.

Beyond GRID

Even though the new disease was called GRID, clinical data showed that the disease was spreading beyond the homosexual community. In early 1982, New York City area hospitals began treating an increasing number of desperately ill Haitians with puzzling symptoms. Some had Pneumocystis carinii pneumonia. A few had the brain infection toxoplasmosis, which is associated with immune system abnormalities. All of these patients insisted that they were heterosexual. Intravenous drug users were also showing T cell abnormalities, regardless of their sexual orientation.

Most frightening of all, people who had received blood transfusions began to show symptoms of immune system breakdown. If the new virus had found its way into the nation's blood supply, then a simple transfusion during routine surgery could become a death sentence. By February 25, 1982, there were twenty-three cases of GRID among heterosexuals, most of whom were intravenous drug users. Their sexual partners also developed the disease, as did an increasing number of prostitutes.

The puzzling Haitian connection could be traced back to Africa. Hundreds of Haitians had worked in

Zaire during the time it was emerging from its colonial past as the Belgian Congo [in 1997 it readopted the name Congo]. There, where the virus is believed to have originated, the disease spread through heterosexual contact. It infected nearly as many women as men. It was fast becoming clear that GRID was not a homosexual disease—it was a human disease.

On July 27, 1982, GRID was given a new name: Acquired Immune Deficiency Syndrome. At that time, 471 cases had been reported to the Centers for Disease Control and Prevention (CDC) in Atlanta, Georgia. Of those cases, 184 people had already died.[2]

The sprawling Centers for Disease Control and Prevention complex in Atlanta, Georgia, where teams of experts work to prevent and contain outbreaks of infectious diseases.

Tracing the Patterns of Death

On March 30, 1984, Gaetan Dugas died, four years after he first noticed the strange purple spot under his ear. By that time, he had become something of a legend as the infamous Patient Zero who supposedly introduced AIDS into North America.

Epidemiological studies of the earliest cases had all traced back to Dugas, placing him at the very center of the gathering storm. There he stayed, apparently by choice rather than by accident. At first, Dugas could not believe he was spreading death with every sexual contact. Like Typhoid Mary Mallon, he refused to let some mysterious infection stop him from living as he pleased.

When he could no longer ignore the truth about his illness, his attitude took a frightening turn. By June 1982, Dugas had become the talk of San Francisco's gay community. People said he was deliberately seeking new sexual partners in order to infect them with AIDS: "'I've got gay cancer,' he'd say [pointing out his KS lesions]. 'I'm going to die and so are you.'"[3] Like plague victims in seventeenth-century London who threw their contaminated bandages at healthy passersby, Dugas struck out at a world he blamed for his misfortune.

On April 24, 1984, less than a month after Dugas died, American virologist Dr. Robert Gallo announced that he had isolated the pathogen responsible for AIDS. He called it Human T-Lymphotropic Virus, Type III (HTLV-III) because he believed it was related to viruses that cause the blood disease leukemia.

Gallo's announcement triggered an international scientific dispute. In the summer of 1983, Dr. Luc Montagnier at the Pasteur Institute in Paris, France, had identified a virus he called Lymphadenopathy-Associated Virus (LAV).

After two years of conflict between the rival researchers, an international panel of scientists made a ruling. They found that HTLV-III was not a leukemia virus but was identical to Dr. Montagnier's LAV. Jonas Salk, of polio vaccine fame, acted as a kind of scientific diplomat to help the two parties arrive at a settlement. Montagnier and Gallo finally agreed to share credit as codiscoverers. Because neither HTLV-III nor LAV was now a suitable name for the virus, it became known as the Human Immunodeficiency Virus (HIV).

Unlike ordinary viruses, HIV is a slow-acting retrovirus that copies its genetic material inside living cells and integrates into their basic structures. In this state, HIV can lie dormant for years. This means that millions of people who have no symptoms of AIDS could be carrying HIV and unknowingly spreading it to others.

By 1985, when blood banks began screening for HIV, twenty-nine thousand people had already been infected through blood transfusions, and twelve thousand hemophiliacs had contracted HIV through blood-clotting products.[4] The worst-case scenario of

Robert Gallo, codiscoverer of the HIV virus, which causes AIDS.

1982 had become the inescapable fact of 1985—
and that was just the beginning.

By 1995, 477,900 Americans had contracted
AIDS and 295,500 had already died. Worldwide,
health authorities estimated that more than 14
million people carried the HIV time bomb locked

within the structures of their cells.[5] The World Health Organization predicts that 40 million people will be infected with HIV by the year 2000.[6]

Public Safety and Individual Rights

As the first known carrier of a deadly disease, Typhoid Mary spent the final years of her life quarantined on an island. No one connected with the case liked this solution, but they did not know what else to do.

If one carrier was a problem, then several million carriers can only be described as a major disaster. When the threat of AIDS became clear in the mid-1980s, people reacted in many ways. Not all of those ways were sensible or humane.

In 1986 Californians voted on a ballot measure that would place all AIDS victims under a strict quarantine. Though the measure was defeated, it left lingering fears in the minds of those infected with HIV. Also in 1986, William F. Buckley, Jr., editor of the conservative *National Review*, said that HIV-positive people should be tattooed on the arm and the buttocks.

Fortunately, cooler heads prevailed.

The fight against HIV and AIDS gained strength in the mid-1990s. In June 1996 researchers announced successful clinical trials of a drug combination that appeared to accomplish the impossible. It reduced HIV to nondetectable levels in infected people. "If you would have asked me in January, 1996, 'Can you eradicate [entirely destroy] HIV infection?' I would have laughed in your face," said Dr. Julio Montaner of the University of British Columbia. "But now we've been able to demonstrate that we can effectively suppress viral production. And this is leading to a dramatic change in how we think of this disease."[7]

Scientists are not sure, however, that the change produced by the new drug combination is permanent. Retroviruses have been known to hide in infected systems—and nobody knows how long they are capable of remaining hidden. By mid-1996, some patients had been free of detectable HIV levels for two years. This is cause for hope, but it is not the final answer to HIV and AIDS.

Treatment with the new drugs is expensive and requires access to high-quality medical care. This means that people in developing countries will probably not have access to the latest treatments. HIV will then join a long list of diseases that run wild in some areas while they have almost disappeared in others.

Despite the hard realities of public health and medical research, the work goes on. Scientists believe that if HIV can be indefinitely suppressed, then perhaps in time it can be eradicated.

Time is critical. For researchers, the conquest of AIDS is a professional challenge. For the millions who are infected with HIV, it is a matter of life and death.

9

The Microbe Hunters

Whatever may happen with AIDS in the future, the fact that a disease no one had heard of until 1980 could do so much damage in a few years has been a wake-up call for medical science. No longer do we wonder if there will be another pandemic, we only wonder when it will strike and what form it will take.

In the last decades of the twentieth century there have been plenty of candidates, ranging from a disease that can transform healthy lungs into waterlogged sacks in a matter of hours to deadly hemorrhagic (bleeding) fevers with names like

100

Lassa, Machupo, and Guanarito, to even deadlier diseases caused by a brand-new life form, the filovirus. We have seen "flesh-eating" disease, mad cow disease, lyme disease, and just to keep things interesting, drug-resistant forms of old enemies such as tuberculosis, cholera, and rabies.

Deadly "Threads"

In 1967, several workers at a pharmaceutical plant in Marburg, Germany, became violently ill. Their illness began with flulike symptoms, then it quickly became something that no one had ever seen before. The victims developed headaches, vomiting, diarrhea, enlarged spleens, and swollen lymph nodes. As the virus progressed, the victims suffered internal bleeding. Their internal organs broke down and blood oozed from every opening in their bodies. The disease became known as Marburg.

It soon turned up in Frankfurt, Germany, and Belgrade, Yugoslavia. In all, thirty-one people became desperately ill with this mysterious illness. Seven of those people died. All of the victims had one thing in common: They had been in contact with African green monkeys. Some worked in animal handling facilities, others in laboratories where the green monkeys were used for research.

In August 1967, German medical authorities sent blood samples to virologist David Simpson at the Porton Down Maximum Security Laboratory in England. Simpson was an experienced researcher, but he could not have been prepared for his first encounter with the Marburg virus.

The virus was unlike anything he had ever seen before, unlike anything anyone had seen. Simpson had discovered a new life form called a filovirus, from the Latin for "thread." It is one of the deadliest microorganisms on earth. According to science writer Richard Preston,

> The filoviruses . . . resemble no other virus on earth.While most viruses are ball-shaped particles that look like peppercorns, the thread viruses have been compared to strands of tangled rope, to hair, to worms, to snakes. When they appear in a great flooding mess, as they so often do when they have destroyed a victim, they look like a tub of spaghetti that has been dumped on the floor. Marburg particles sometimes roll up into loops. . . . Marburg is the only ring-shaped virus known.[1]

After more than thirty years of study, much about the filoviruses remains a mystery. Scientists know what a filovirus looks like and what it does. What they do not know is exactly how it does those things.

"It's Not Marburg"

In the summer of 1976, a Sudanese worker known to medical historians as Mr. Yu.G. became violently ill and died with blood running from his eyes and ears and leaking from the pores of his skin. Beyond the obvious fact that it was some kind of hemorrhagic fever, no one knew exactly what had killed Yu.G.

A few days after his death, two of Yu.G.'s co-workers also became sick and died. Later, the virus found its way into a hospital in the town of Maridi. "It hit the hospital like a bomb," according to Preston.

> As it jumped from bed to bed, killing patients left and right, doctors began to notice signs of mental derangement . . . [and] zombie-like behavior. Some of the dying stripped off their clothes and ran out of the hospital, naked and bleeding . . . not seeming to know what had happened or how they had gotten into this condition.[2]

This description sounds like something from Thucydides' account of the smallpox epidemic in ancient Athens: victims delirious with sickness, wandering mindlessly until they fall over dead. Although these epidemics are separated by twenty-five hundred years and caused by different germs, both show the disastrous impact a pathogen can have when it strikes a virgin population.

While epidemiologists were busy with the Sudan outbreak, another epidemic struck five hundred miles away in the country then known as Zaire. In and around the Yambuku Hospital, people were becoming sick and were dying at an alarming rate.

Studies of the Zaire and Sudan outbreaks revealed as the culprit a virus that looked suspiciously familiar—it resembled a thread. The word Marburg came up in every laboratory discussion. Viral pathologist Patricia Webb was assigned to confirm this educated guess with experimental evidence. What she found instead was terrifying: "It's not Marburg," Webb told her colleagues.[3]

It was a new filovirus, and it was even deadlier than Marburg. Webb's discovery became known as Ebola, after the river that flowed through the rain forest where it was found. In time, the microbe hunters realized that there were two distinct strains of Ebola: *Ebola Zaire* and *Ebola Sudan*. The Sudan virus killed half of the people it infected, a death rate equaled only by the Black Death of the fourteenth century. Ebola Zaire was even worse, killing 90 percent of its victims.

The virus, which Richard Preston calls "a molecular shark," can transform "virtually every part of the body into a digested slime of virus particles."[4] It kills piece by piece, while the victim is still alive, triggering "a creeping, spotty necrosis [death of tissue in a living animal; gangrene] that spreads through all the internal organs."[5]

Both strains burn themselves out before spreading to major population centers. "The Ebola virus is ill-suited to sustaining an epidemic: it kills victims so quickly that they don't have much chance to infect others," wrote journalist Michael D. Lemonick in 1995.[6]

Ebola Zaire staged a brief but frightening comeback in the town of Kikwit in 1995, killing 245 of the 318 people it infected.[7] Only the swift lethality of Ebola Zaire, along with the fact that it can only be spread through direct contact, have prevented it from turning into some kind of doomsday virus.

The Virus with No Name

The Four Corners area is where the states of Arizona, New Mexico, Colorado, and Utah meet. It is a place of buttes and gorges and pastel deserts. Here, in the homeland of the Navajo Nation, a fearsome disease appeared as if from nowhere.

The story of the Four Corners epidemic begins with two young people, usually identified only by their first names, "Merrill," or sometimes "Michael," and "Rosina." They were healthy, athletic young Navajo with bright futures ahead of them.

In the spring of 1993, they were busy planning their wedding. On May 4, however, Rosina began feeling sick with what appeared to be the flu. When this "flu" kept getting worse, she was taken to the hospital. Less than two days later she died of respiratory failure.

On May 14, Merrill was on his way to her funeral when he became violently ill. He began feeling sick around 9 A.M., with fever, muscle aches, and stabbing pains in his chest. "The deterioration was frighteningly rapid," wrote Dr. Frank Ryan. "Within ten or fifteen minutes, his hands and lips were blue and he was gasping for breath."[8]

Merrill was rushed by ambulance to the Indian Health Service hospital in Gallup, New Mexico. Despite desperate efforts to resuscitate him, Merrill died at 11:53 A.M., less than three hours after he was first stricken. When doctors examined the body, there was no question about the cause of Merrill's death: His lungs were like waterlogged sponges.

The tragedy of Merrill and Rosina was only the beginning. By May 25 epidemiologist Rob Breimen had found nineteen cases in the Four Corners area. Twelve of them had died. "Within a matter of hours patients would become . . . unable to absorb [the] oxygen that they hungrily inhaled," writes author Laurie Garrett. "Starving for oxygen, the heart would slow down and death could soon follow, caused by either cardiac [heart] failure or pulmonary edema [swelling of the lungs]."[9]

Community Reaction

Lethal epidemics have a way of bringing out the worst in people, as history has so often shown. When news reports branded the outbreak a "Navajo disease," fear of contagion aroused old prejudices. Non-Indians avoided Navajo businesses and even Navajo friends. Tourists drove through the Four Corners area with gauze surgical masks over their faces. Waitresses put on rubber gloves before they would serve Navajo customers.

Worst of all, gangs of thugs roamed the border towns, beating up any Navajo they could find. It was reminiscent of the way mobs attacked Jews and other outsiders during the Great Dying of the four-teenth century.

The Navajo reacted by banning the media from

their land. They almost banned the epidemiologists who came to track down the epidemic. Fortunately, the CDC team was able to convince Navajo leaders to allow the investigation.

By June 3, Dr. C.J. Peters, then head of the Special Pathogens branch of CDC, had identified the Four Corners pathogen as a strain of hantavirus. This virus family first surfaced in the early 1950s. It struck American and Korean soldiers fighting in the region of the Hantaan River during the Korean War. The U.S. Army Medical Research Institute of Infectious Diseases (USAMRIID) traced the outbreak to its host animal: a field mouse that was common throughout the Hantaan river area.

The culprit at Four Corners was the deer mouse, a creature "so cute-looking it could appear in a Disney nature film."[10] Health authorities quickly launched rodent control measures to stop the epidemic at its source. They also used an experimental antiviral drug called ribavirin to treat victims of the disease. Naming the new strain of hantavirus was unexpectedly difficult. The Navajo Nation rejected "Four Corners" because the name was so closely associated with their people.

Peters proposed the name "Muerto Canyon," after the dry gully near where the first victims died. This time the National Park Service objected, "because it already had a location called Canyon del Muerto—Canyon of the Dead—in Arizona, and felt an association with a deadly virus could be bad for tourism," Peters writes. "Finally, after mulling over many more possibilities, we came up with a name everyone could live with. . . . The Sin Nombre virus, or the No Name virus. For the killer without a name."[11]

Millennium: Disease in the Global Village

In the last two decades of the twentieth century, the relationship between humankind and microbes has begun to look like a script for a horror movie. Not only is there AIDS and Ebola, but there is also a gruesome flesh-eating bacteria that transforms living tissue into rotting patches of gangrene; mad cow disease, a fatal brain infection that can pass from cattle to humans; and a return of old enemies like tuberculosis and cholera.

Health organizations throughout the world maintain constant readiness. Quick response to an outbreak can make the difference between containment and worldwide disaster. The World Health Organization monitors epidemics on a worldwide scale. In the United States, that job falls to a special division of the CDC, the National Center for Infectious Diseases (NCID).

Every organism NCID studies is infectious to one degree or another. So the first objective with any biohazard (dangerous organism) is to make sure it cannot spread beyond the laboratory. To reduce this danger as much as possible, NCID has created a system of containment procedures for its research laboratories. There are different levels of containment, called Biosafety Levels (BSL).

A "glove box" at the Centers for Disease Control and Prevention high-contaminant laboratory enables researchers to keep infectious material isolated during experiments.

Organisms are grouped within these levels according to how deadly and how contagious they are.

BSL-2 diseases (there is no BSL-1) are contagious but rarely deadly. Measles, mumps, and influenza fall into this class. BSL-3 diseases are both deadly and highly contagious, but there are vaccines to protect against most of them. BSL-3 diseases include yellow fever and anthrax. Workers in both levels 2 and 3 are required to have long series of vaccinations.

Workers in BSL-4, however, are not required to have any special vaccinations. The reason is the organisms in this level are the most frightening killers known to science. No vaccine can prevent them, and no drug or treatment can cure them. BSL-4 is reserved for the likes of Ebola and hantavirus.

A BSL-4 laboratory is a medical fortress. Air is filtered and refiltered before being released to the outside. Water is boiled. Workers wear "biological space suits" with sealed helmets and individual air supplies. These suits are hot and bulky. Incoming air hisses so loudly that workers have trouble hearing one another. Everyone who works in BSL-4 containment knows that just walking into the laboratory puts his or her life at risk. They also know that theirs is an uphill struggle; microbes are far more adaptable than humans can ever hope to be.

Microbes breed new generations in a matter of minutes, changing and adapting as they grow. An organism that is spread through direct contact can become an airborne pathogen, becoming even more contagious. Likewise, an organism that lives in an animal or insect host can "jump" to human beings.

Microbes can also become resistant to drugs that once killed them. Even the best "wonder drug" cannot kill every microbe in a population; a few will always survive to pass on their resistant genes. The result is a newer, tougher "super bug" that cannot be destroyed by previous methods.

In the 1990s, rabies made a comeback in New York State, infecting more than three thousand people a year. In California, tuberculosis struck one

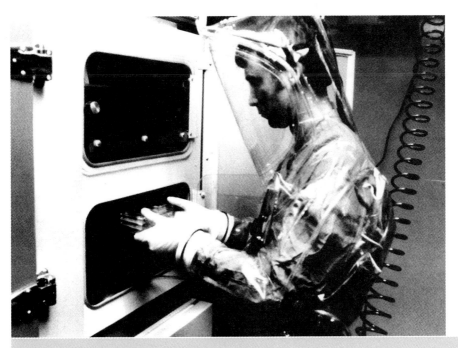

Isolation suits with independent air supplies protect researchers when they must enter a "hot room."

third of the students at a Los Angeles high school, some with a new strain that did not respond to standard treatments.

Sometimes, returning pathogens branch out to infect new host species. Rabies spread to coyotes and raccoons in New York State. The E. coli bacterium, which causes food poisoning, once appeared only in meat; in 1995, it began showing up in fruits and vegetables. An outbreak of E. coli in Massachusetts was traced back to unpasteurized apple juice; one in California was caused by contaminated strawberries.

Epidemiologists often wonder what will be the next killer plague, trying to determine what form it might take, where it might strike, and how many it might kill. In addition to these global dangers, hundreds of smaller, more localized epidemics strike every year, bringing death and misery into people's lives.

A month after meningitis killed fifteen-year-old Heather Ziese, it struck another young woman in the Sacramento area. On the morning of April 10, 1997, twenty-five-year-old Stephanie McCullough began vomiting violently. Ten minutes after arriving at a hospital emergency room, she lost consciousness and was placed on life-support machines. She died a week later.

The bacteria that cause meningitis live in the nasal passages of 10 to 25 percent of the population.[12] What makes this normally harmless microbe turn deadly? Epidemiologists still do not know. In the age of AIDS and Ebola there are many unanswered questions, but one fact is clear: The struggle against infectious disease is far from over. The prevention, cure, and control of disease will continue to require dedication, ongoing effort—and now and then a streak of luck.

Chapter Notes

Chapter 1. Demons, Miasmas, and Microbes

1. Quoted in Tom Philip, "Student Apparent Meningitis Victim," *Sacramento Bee*, March 13, 1997, p. A1.

2. Board of Trustees, University of Illinois, 1995.

3. Centers for Disease Control and Prevention, "Summary of Notifiable Diseases, United States, 1995," *MMWR 1995*, 44 (53), table 2, p. 74.

4. Laurie Garrett, *The Coming Plague: Newly Emerging Diseases in a World out of Balance* (New York: Farrar, Straus and Giroux, 1994), p. 65.

5. World Health Organization, "Interagency Appeal to Control Epidemic Meningitis in Africa," press release (Geneva, Switzerland: World Health Organization, February 5, 1997), n.p.

6. Shannon Brownlee, "The disease busters," *U.S. News and World Report*, March 27, 1995, pp. 48–50.

7. Arno Karlen, *Man and Microbes: Disease and Plague in History and Modern Times* (New York: G.P. Putnam's Sons, 1995), p. 48.

8. Charles-Edward Amory Winslow, *The Conquest of Epidemic Disease: A Chapter in the History of Ideas* (1943; reprint, Madison: The University of Wisconsin Press, 1980), p. 5.

9. Theodore H. Gaster, *The New Golden Bough: A New Abridgement of the Classic Work by Sir James George Frazer* (New York: New American Library, 1964), p. 598.

10. Hippocrates, *On Airs, Waters, and Places*, trans. Francis Adams (Garden Grove, Calif.: Library of the Future CD-Rom, 1991), screens 1–2.

Chapter 2. The Black Death

1. Bacterial Zoonoses Branch, Division of Vector-borne Infectious Diseases, "Plague Information: Health-care Worker Information" (Fort Collins, Colo.: Centers for Disease Control and Prevention, March 9, 1995), n.p.

2. Ibid., n.p.

3. Barbara W. Tuchman, *A Distant Mirror: The Calamitous 14th Century* (New York: Knopf, 1978), p. 99.

4. Quoted in Philip Ziegler, *The Black Death* (Dover, N.H.: Alan Sutton Publishing Inc., 1993), p. 67.

Chapter 3. Predators at Large

1. Arno Karlen, *Man and Microbes: Disease and Plague in History and Modern Times* (New York: G.P. Putnam's Sons, 1995), p. 16.

2. Ibid., p. 103.

3. Thucydides, *The History of the Peloponnesian War*, trans. Richard Crawley, Second Book, Chapter 7. Books on Line, n.d., <http://classics.mit.edu/Thucydides/pelopwar.html> (n.p.).

4. Ibid.

5. Quoted in Robin Marantz Henig, "The Lessons of Syphilis in the Age of AIDS," *Civilization*, vol. 2, November/December 1995, pp. 36–43.

6. Daniel Defoe, *A Journal of the Plague Year*, Project Gutenberg, n.d., <http://ulserver.speech.cs.cmu.edu/gutenberg/etext95/jplag10.txt> (n.p.).

7. Ibid.

8. Ibid.

9. Quoted in Walter George Bell, *The Great Plague of London* (1924; reprint, London: Bracken Books, 1994), p. 233.

10. Ibid., p. 325.

11. Defoe, ibid.

12. Bell, ibid., p. 52.

Chapter 4. Brave New Worlds

1. Quoted in Arno Karlen, *Man and Microbes: Disease and Plague in History and Modern Times* (New York: G.P. Putnam's Sons, 1995), p. 102.

2. Quoted in C.C. O'Mally, ed., *The History of Medical Education* (Berkeley: University of California Press, 1970), p. 464.

3. Karlen, ibid., p. 105.

4. Ibid., p. 85.

5. World Health Organization, "World TB Day: March 24, 1997," press release (Geneva, Switzerland: World Health Organization), n.p.

6. Laurie Garrett, *The Coming Plague: Newly Emerging Diseases in a World out of Balance* (New York: Farrar, Straus and Giroux, 1994), p. 66.

7. Quoted in Charles-Edward Amory Winslow, *The Conquest of Epidemic Disease: A Chapter in the History of Ideas* (1943; reprint, Madison: The University of Wisconsin Press, 1980), p. 199.

Chapter 5. Turning Points

1. Charles-Edward Amory Winslow, *The Conquest of Epidemic Disease: A Chapter in the History of Ideas* (1943; reprint, Madison: The University of Wisconsin Press, 1980), p. 249.

2. Bayard Taylor, *Eldorado or Adventures in the Path of Empire* (1949; reprint, Lincoln: University of Nebraska Press, 1988), p. 213.

3. Sarah Royce, *A Frontier Lady: Recollections of the Gold Rush and Early California* (1932; reprint, Lincoln: University of Nebraska Press, 1977), p. 15.

4. Robert Ginsberg, "John Snow Is Remembered with a Pump—At the Scene," *Nation's Health*, vol. 22, September 1992, p. 31.

Chapter 6. Stalking the Enemy

1. Hans Zisser, *Rats, Lice and History* (1934; reprint, New York: Black Dog & Leventhal Publishers, 1996), p. 41.

2. Louis Pasteur, "Germ Theory and Its Applications to Medicine and Surgery," *Great Works of Literature*, trans. H.C. Ernst, Electric Library, 1997, <http://www.elibrary.com> (n.p.).

3. Quoted in Charles-Edward Amory Winslow, *The Conquest of Epidemic Disease: A Chapter in the History of Ideas* (1943; reprint, Madison: University of Wisconsin Press, 1980), p. 308.

4. Ronald Reese, "Under the Weather," *History Today*, vol. 46, Electric Library, <http://www.elibrary.com> (January 1, 1996).

Chapter 7. Adventures in Medical Detection: 1900–1950

1. Alan M. Kraut, *Silent Travelers: Germs, Genes, and the "Immigrant Menace"* (Baltimore: Johns Hopkins University Press, 1994), p. 52.

2. Quoted in Richmond Mayo-Smith, *Emigration and Immigration: A Study in Social Science* (New York: Scribner's, 1890), p. 133.

3. Manly H. Simons, "The Origin and Condition of the Peoples Who Make Up the Bulk of Our Immigrants at the Present Time and the Probable Effect of the Absorption upon Our Population," *The Military Surgeon*, December 23, 1908, p. 433.

4. S. Josephine Baker, *Fighting for Life* (New York: Macmillan, 1939), p. 74.

5. Ibid., pp. 74–75.

6. Ibid., p. 75.

7. Ibid., p. 76.

8. Ibid.

9. Judith Walzer Leavitt, *Typhoid Mary: Captive to the Public's Health* (Boston: Beacon Press, 1996), pp. 253–254.

10. Sherwin B. Nuland, "A Summer Plague: Polio and Its Survivors," *The New Republic*, vol. 213, October 15, 1995, pp. 47–52.

11. Ibid.

12. Ibid.

13. Associated Press release, "From Rare Meeting of Two Viruses, Killer Flu May Prey on Millions," *Sacramento Bee*, December 17, 1995, p. A6.

14. Alfred W. Crosby, *America's Forgotten Pandemic: The Influenza of 1918* (Cambridge, Mass.: Cambridge University Press, 1989).

Chapter 8. The Age of AIDS

1. Quoted in Robin Marantz Henig, "The Lessons of Syphilis in the Age of AIDS," *Civilization*, November/December 1995, p. 36.

2. Randy Shilts, *And the Band Played On* (New York: St. Martin's, 1987), p. 168.

3. Ibid., p. 165.

4. Michael Chapman, "Politics Infects the Nation's Blood Supply," *Human Events*, vol. 50, May 27, 1994, p. 12.

5. "Acquired Immune Deficiency Syndrome (AIDS)," *Colliers Encyclopedia, Electric Library*, 1995, <http://www.elibrary.com> (n.p.).

6. Kim Painter, "A Time Line of the Epidemic's Spread," *USA Today*, June 5, 1996, p. 5D.

7. Quoted in Laurie Garrett, "New AIDS Hope/Drugs, Tests Seen as Way to 'Eradicate' Virus from Body," *Newsday*, June 14, 1996, p. A4.

Chapter 9. The Microbe Hunters

1. Richard Preston, *The Hot Zone* (New York: Random House, 1994), p. 37.

2. Ibid., p. 98.

3. Quoted in Frank Ryan, *Tracking the New Killer Plagues: Out of the Present and into the Future* (Boston: Little, Brown and Co., 1997), p. 173.

4. Preston, ibid., p. 105.

5. Ibid., p. 107.

6. Michael D. Lemonick, "Medicine: Return to the Hot Zone: The gruesome Ebola virus, dormant for 16 years, has arisen to kill again in Zaire. Will it spread?" *Time*, May 22, 1995, pp. 62–63.

7. Marlene Cimons, "Medical Detectives Hunt for Killer Virus' Hide-out," *Press-Democrat* (Santa Rosa, Calif.), July 15, 1996, p. A6.

8. Ryan, ibid., p. 17.

9. Laurie Garrett, *The Coming Plague: Newly Emerging Diseases in a World out of Balance* (New York: Farrar, Straus and Giroux, 1994), p. 534.

10. C.J. Peters and Mark Olshaker, "Virus Hunter," *Reader's Digest*, April 1997, p. 236.

11. Ibid., p. 243.

12. Cynthia Hubert, "Meningitis Strikes Again— Placer Waitress Dies," *Sacramento Bee*, April 19, 1997, p. B1.

Further Reading

Fisher, Jeffrey. *The Plague Makers*. New York: Simon & Schuster, 1994. Discusses how microbes develop into drug resistant "super bugs."

Giblin, James C. *When Plague Strikes: The Black Death, Smallpox, AIDS*. New York: HarperCollins Children's Books, 1995.

Henig, Robin. *A Dancing Matrix: Voyages Along the Viral Frontier*. New York: Knopf, 1993. An overview of modern virus hunters.

Hyde, Margaret O. and Elizabeth H. Forsyth. *The Disease Book*. New York: Walker & Company, 1997.

Lamond, Margrete. *Plague & Pestilence: Deadly Diseases That Changed the World*. Chicago: Independent Publishers Group, 1997.

Majure, Janet. *AIDS*. Springfield, N.J.: Enslow Publishers, Inc., 1998.

Radetsky, Peter. *The Invisible Invaders*. Boston: Little, Brown and Co., 1991.

Regis, Edward. *Virus Ground Zero: Stalking the Killer Viruses with the Centers for Disease Control*. New York: Pocket Books, 1996. A chronicle of the Ebola Zaire outbreak of 1995.

Roden, Katie. *Plague*. Brookfield, Conn.: Millbrook Press, 1996.

Ryan, Frank. *The Forgotten Plague*. Boston: Little, Brown and Co., 1993. The author of Virus X traces the history and reemergence of tuberculosis.

Silverstein, Alvin, Virginia, & Robert. *Tuberculosis*. Springfield, N.J.: Enslow Publishers, Inc., 1994.

Zinsser, Hans. *Rats, Lice & History*. New York: Little, Brown & Company, 1984.

On the Internet

Centers for Disease Control and Prevention home page

<http://www.cdc.gov>

The mission of the CDC is to promote health and quality of life by preventing and controlling disease, injury, and disability. The Centers for Disease Control and Prevention (CDC) Web page provides health links and information to promote awareness and prevention.

Health Canada home page

<http://hwcweb.hwc.ca>

Health Canada's mission is to help the people of Canada maintain and improve their health. By providing links to sites such as the Laboratory Centre for Disease Control, this page offers essential health information to the people of Canada.

Johns Hopkins Medical Institution Information Network

<http://infonet.welch.jhu.edu>

The Johns Hopkins Medical Institution InfoNet lists the names and addresses and provides links to organizations that help prevent and cure infectious diseases.

Laboratory Centre for Disease Control-Canada home page

<http://hwcweb.hwc.ca/hpb/lcdc/hc_eng.html>

The Laboratory Centre for Disease Control is Canada's national center for the identification, investigation, prevention, and control of human disease.

National Center for Infectious Diseases home page

<http://www.cdc.gov/ncidod/ncid.htm>

The mission of the NDIC is to prevent illness, disability, and death caused by infectious diseases in the United States and around the world. The NDIC Web page offers publications and resources that provide information to prevent the emergence and spread of infectious diseases.

National Institutes of Health home page

<http://www.nih.gov>

The National Institutes of Health is dedicated to

uncovering new knowledge that will lead to better health for everyone. By providing links and information on sites dedicated to specific diseases, the NIH home page aids in the fight against infectious disease.

National Library of Medicine home page

<http://www.nlm.nih.gov>

The National Library of Medicine is the world's largest research library in a single scientific and professional field. The NLM Web page offers vast resources, including information and historical archives on plagues and infectious diseases.

Index

About the Author

Linda Jacobs Altman is the author of more than fifteen books for young people on history, social issues, and multicultural subjects. Among the books she has written for Enslow Publishers, Inc., are *The Holocaust Ghettos*, *Genocide: The Systematic Killing of a People*, and *The California Gold Rush in American History*.